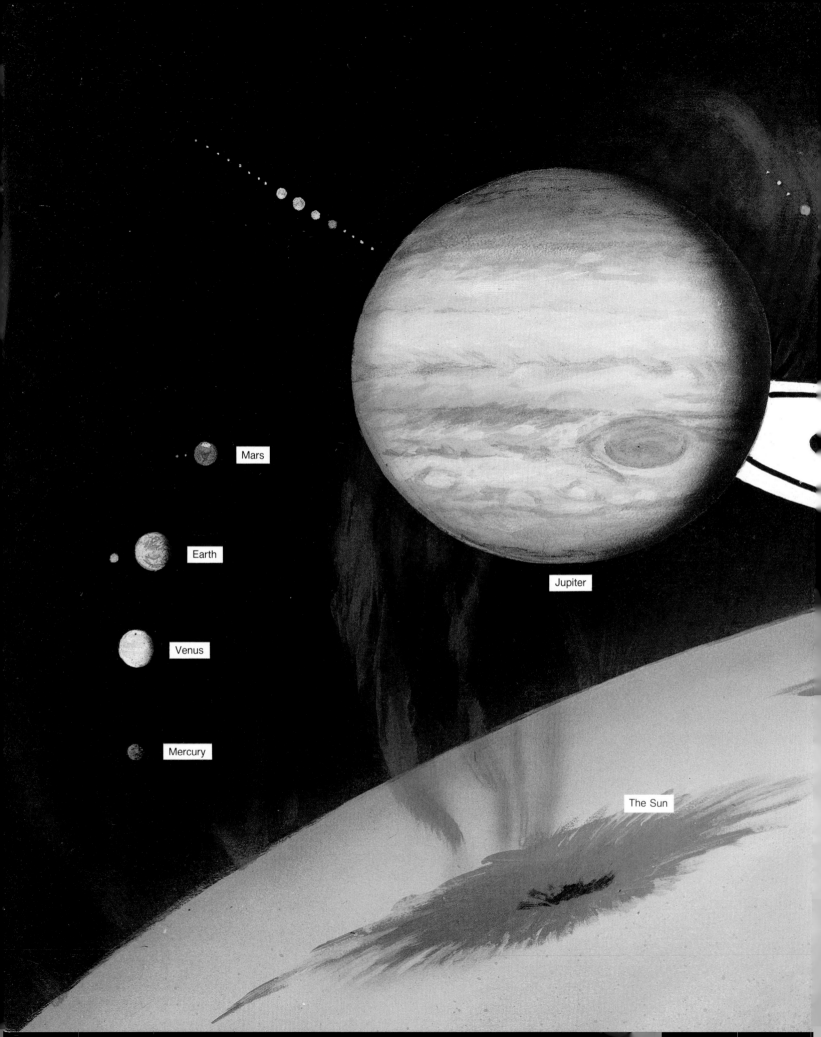

Rand McNally
Children's
Atlas of the
World

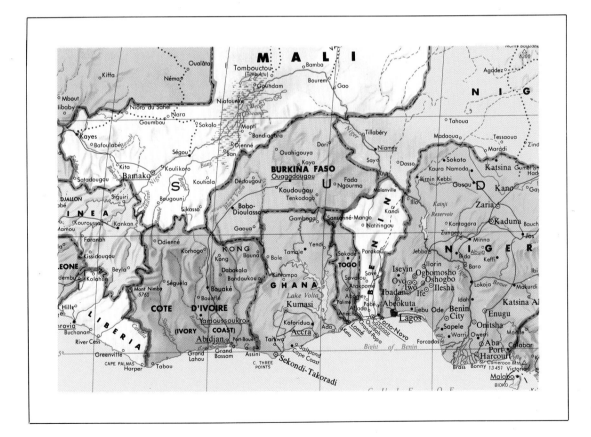

Peafowl

Gibbon

Cobra

Rand McNally Children's Atlas of the World

General manager: Russell L. Voisin
Managing editor: Jon M. Leverenz
Editor: Elizabeth Fagan Adelman
Production editor: Laura C. Schmidt
Manufacturing planner: Marianne Abraham

Rand McNally Children's Atlas of the World
Copyright © 1994 by Rand McNally & Company

Photograph Credits
Pages 6-7: Pakistan/Ric Ergenbright; Alps/Rand McNally Pictorial
World Atlas. **22-23:** Alps/Rand McNally Pictorial World Atlas;
County Kerry/Ric Ergenbright; Mikonos/Rand McNally Student's
World Atlas. **29:** Eiffel Tower/Joe Viesti. **34:** China and Paki-
stan/Ric Ergenbright. **40 and cover:** Jerusalem/Rand McNally Pic-
torial World Atlas, Colour Library International Limited. **44-45:**
Zambia/Rand McNally Atlas of Mankind; Gulf of Guinea/Anna
Tully, Hutchinson Picture Library. **50 and cover:** Masai/Rand Mc-
Nally Children's World Atlas; **51:** Tunisia/R.G. Williamson, Tele-
graph Colour Library; Zimbabwe/Christopher Arnesen, Allstock.
56-57: Australia/Robert Ivey, Ric Ergenbright Photography; New
Caledonia/ Christopher Arnesen, Allstock. **64-65:** Caribbe-
an/Nathan Benn, Allstock; Monument Valley and British Colum-
bia/Ric Ergenbright. **70-71 and cover:** Mexico City/Rand McNally
Pictorial World Atlas; Washington D.C./Art Wolfe, Allstock. **78-
79:** Peru/Ric Ergenbright; Guyana/Hutchinson Picture Library;
Paraguay/Peter Keen, Telegraph Colour Library. **84-85:** Surina-
me/R. Phillips, Image Bank; Rio de Janerio/Robert Ivey, Ric
Ergenbright Photography; Ecuador/Rand McNally Pictorial World
Atlas. **89:** Antarctica/Rand McNally Pictorial World Atlas.

Every effort has been made to trace the copyright holders of the
photographs in this publication. Rand McNally apologizes in advance for any unintentional omissions and would be pleased to
insert the appropriate acknowledgment in any subsequent edition
of this book.

Library of Congress Cataloging-in-Publication Data

Rand McNally and Company.
    Children's atlas of the world. -- Rev. ed.
        p.   cm.
    Includes index.
    ISBN 0-528-83541-6
    1. Children's atlases. [1. Atlases. 2. Geography.]
    I. Title.
G1021.R28   1994   < G&M >
912--dc20
                                93-41313
                                    CIP
                                MAP AC

Contents

Our Planet Earth
A World of Terrain

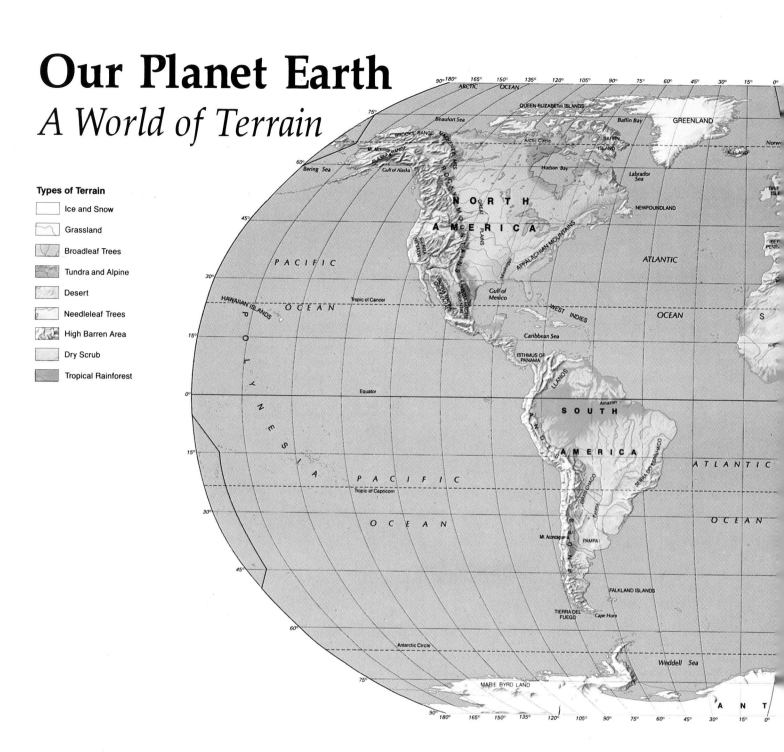

Types of Terrain

	Ice and Snow
	Grassland
	Broadleaf Trees
	Tundra and Alpine
	Desert
	Needleleaf Trees
	High Barren Area
	Dry Scrub
	Tropical Rainforest

This map shows the world's *terrain*, or the different types of land that can be found on the surface of the earth. The colors and shading of the areas on the map indicate the kind of terrain found in that area of the world. The *legend* to the left of the map explains what the colors mean.

The earth's surface is a wrinkled layer of solid rock called the *crust*, which constantly changes. The crust is cracked into a dozen separate fragments called *tectonic plates*, which float on a sea of dense, semi-liquid rock far below. Columns of this molten rock slowly rise and fall within the earth, nudging the bases of the crustal plates that float on the surface. As the plates try to move, they push into their neighbors.

Sometimes two plates may lock together as they grind past one another. Pressure builds in the rock over many years; then suddenly the rock shatters and the plates slip. This movement creates earthquakes. Volcanoes rumble to

life when molten rock from the interior of the earth finds its way to the surface.

Over millions of years, the pushing and grinding of tectonic plates has crumpled, folded, and lifted rock, slowly building up the world's great mountain ranges in million-year-long collisions between the continents. For instance, the Appalachian Mountains that run along North America's eastern coast are the result of a collision with Africa that occurred some 320 million years ago. Likewise, the Himalayas, the highest mountains of the world, were forced upward when India rammed into Asia. On this map, you can easily see where the earth's mountains are.

The map also clearly shows the world's desert regions. Deserts are dry lands with low rainfall and sparse plant and animal life. Not all deserts are hot, sandy, and sunny. They can also be cold, rocky, or ice covered.

A World of Climate

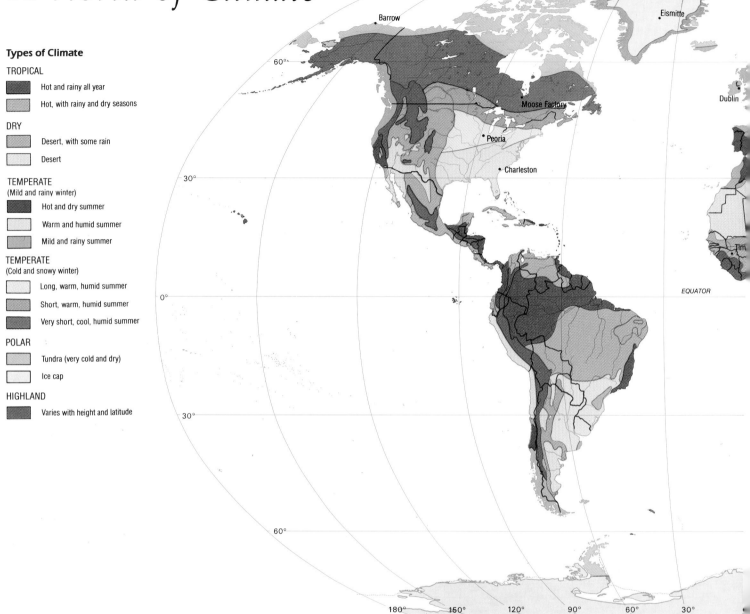

Types of Climate

TROPICAL
- Hot and rainy all year
- Hot, with rainy and dry seasons

DRY
- Desert, with some rain
- Desert

TEMPERATE
(Mild and rainy winter)
- Hot and dry summer
- Warm and humid summer
- Mild and rainy summer

TEMPERATE
(Cold and snowy winter)
- Long, warm, humid summer
- Short, warm, humid summer
- Very short, cool, humid summer

POLAR
- Tundra (very cold and dry)
- Ice cap

HIGHLAND
- Varies with height and latitude

This map shows the climates of the world. The colors of the different areas on the map tell you the kind of climate found in that area of the world. The legend to the left of the map will help you match the map's colors to the type of climate.

Climate and weather are not the same thing. *Weather* describes the temperature and *precipitation*—rain, snow, or other moisture—of an area during a short time. Climate, on the other hand, describes the same things but for a much longer period of time. It takes many years to determine a region's climate.

The climate we live in directly affects our lifestyles.

From the types of clothing we wear to the kind of food we eat, from the way we travel from one place to another to the kinds of homes we live in—all are dictated by climate.

Climates around the world vary for different reasons. In general, the world's climates are hotter closer to the equator and get colder as you go far-

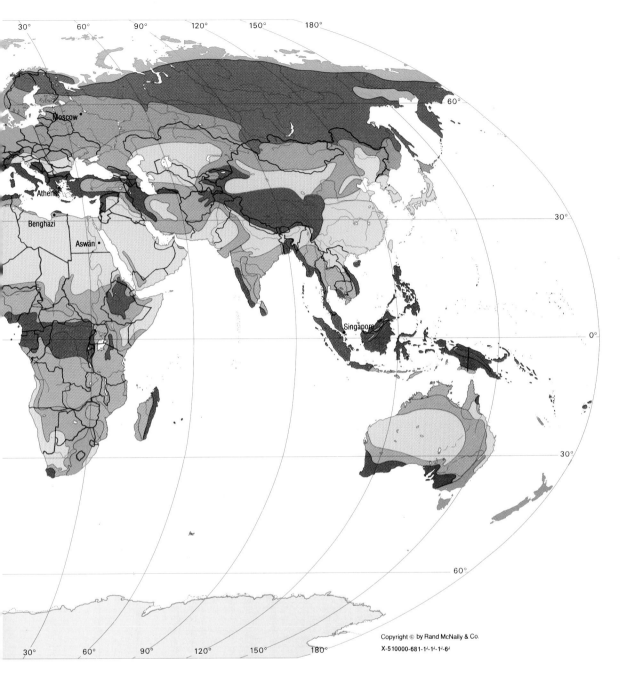

ther north or south. In addition, climates can be affected by large bodies of water, ocean currents, and by the terrain.

Water evaporates from the oceans, rises, cools, forms droplets, and falls as rain onto the land. Usually, the heaviest areas of precipitation in the world are along the equator, where warm, tropical air can hold the greatest amount of water vapor. The reddish areas on the map show the world's tropical climates—the great rain forests of South America, central Africa, and Indonesia lie here, straddling the equator.

Terrain can have a major effect on precipitation. When the terrain assists the rise of moist air, the pattern of rainfall can change dramatically. Mountain ranges force moist air to rise over them, often creating heavy rains on one side of the range and very little on the other. Moist air raised by mountains affects the rainfall in southern Alaska, western Norway, and southern Chile.

OUR PLANET EARTH
A World of Activity

Major Activities

- Manufacturing and trade
- Farming: Raising crops and animals
- Raising animals on rangeland
- Tropical hunting, fishing, food collecting, and primitive farming
- Nomadic animal herding (deserts)
- Forestry; lumber and pulpwood with some hunting and fishing
- Sub-arctic hunting, fishing, food collecting with some forestry
- Animal herding, hunting and fishing
- Important fishing regions
- Little or no economic activity

This map shows the major economic activities of the world. The colors of the different areas on the map tell you what most of the people do for a living in that area of the world. Use the legend as you look at the map.

The character of the land has much to do with its use. In general, the farmed areas shown on the map are among the most fertile on earth. The fertile plains of Europe, southeastern Asia, and central North America feed much of the world's billions. Agriculture occupies most of the working population of India and China. In Brazil and the nations of eastern Europe, a much smaller part of the work force raises crops. And this fraction is smaller still in Canada, the United States, and western Europe.

You can see that very few regions of the world are used for manufacturing and trade. These areas are sometimes called *developed*, and they became developed for a variety of reasons. In the United

States, for instance, many developed areas grew up near natural resources and transportation routes. Major manufacturing centers such as Chicago and Montreal line the shores of the Great Lakes and the St. Lawrence seaway, an important transportation route that provides access to the Atlantic Ocean. Germany has become a major force in European industry. And tiny Japan, smaller than the U.S. state of California, leads Asia with its manufacturing might.

Compare this map to the terrain map. You can often tell what the people in an area of the world do by knowing what the land is like. For example, there is usually a lot of fishing along coastlines. Some of the world's most productive fishing areas include the coasts of North America, Europe, and the eastern coast of Asia. But sometimes you cannot predict what people do by the land on which they live. For example, people may live on good farmland, but they may not be able to farm it efficiently.

A World of People

Population Density
Per square mile

	Uninhabited
	Under 2 inhabitants
	2-25 inhabitants
	25-60 inhabitants
	60-125 inhabitants
	125-250 inhabitants
	Over 250 inhabitants
•	Metropolitan areas over 2,000,000 population
○	Metropolitan areas 1,000,000 to 2,000,000 population

This map shows where people live. Different colors tell you how many people are found in that area of the world. The legend tells you what the colors mean in terms of *population density*. This is a measure of the number of people living in each square mile (2.59 square kilometers) of land.

Naturally, population densities vary for many reasons, including climate and terrain. For example, the continent of Antarctica—the coldest region on Earth—is *uninhabited*, meaning that no one lives there permanently. The harsh climate makes settlement nearly impossible.

Lands with favorable cli-mates and terrains tend to be densely populated, especially if they are good for farming. The ribbon of dense population that runs north through the desert lands of Sudan and Egypt is explained by the Nile River. The people here stay close to its fertile shores. In South America, in the vast rain forest, people settle along

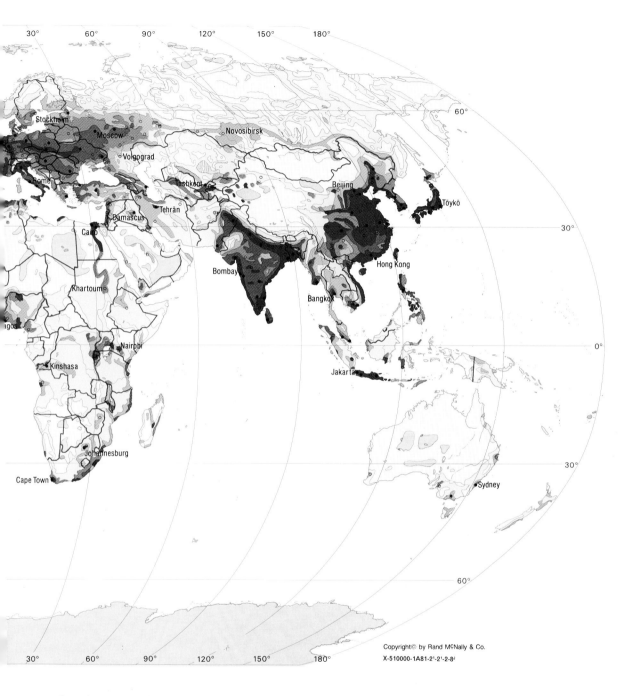

the Amazon River.

Look for the red and purple regions—the world's most thickly populated areas. The huge populations of India and China mostly live in the regions' rich farmlands. In such countries as China, India, and Turkey most of the people still live in country, or *rural*, areas away from cities.

In Europe and the United States, the most populous areas— the cities, or *urban* areas—grew up near farmland, resources, and trade routes, especially waterways. In the United States, the population is concentrated along the northeastern coast, the shores of the Great Lakes, and the banks of the Mississippi,

and along the West Coast. Cities hold the greatest part of the population of Australia, Argentina, Canada, France, Japan, and the United States.

One of the world's most densely populated nations is Japan. This country is slightly smaller than the state of California but holds a population of over 124 million people.

OUR PLANET EARTH
A World of Nations

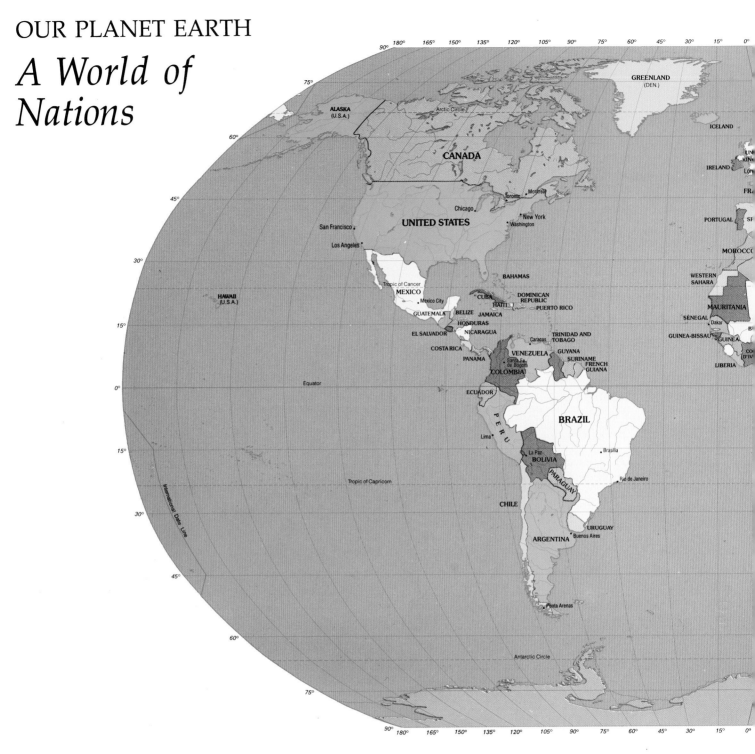

This map shows the countries of the earth. The colors simply make it easier to see each separate country on the map; they do not tell you anything about each nation. This type of map is called *political* because it shows the world's political divisions.

National borders are represented on the map as thin red lines. These lines divide the world into separate countries. Sometimes they follow natural formations such as mountain ranges or rivers. For example, the crooked northwestern border of China runs along a river. In some cases, though, the line is designated by humans—as with the straight portion of the border between Canada and the United States.

Although most political borders in today's world are well established, changes still occur. In 1990, for instance, East and West Germany united, and Germany became a single nation. In 1991, the Soviet Union dissolved, and many nations that had been a part of the union became independent.

Some countries are large, and some countries are small. Russia and Canada are huge nations. The world's smallest independent state is Vatican City, in Rome, Italy.

When people study the world, they often organize all the countries by land areas called *continents*. The seven continents are the great divisions of the earth. Nearly all of them are large pieces of land that are almost completely surrounded by water.

This atlas divides the world into the seven continents: Europe, Asia, Africa, North America, South America, Antarctica, and the area in the South Pacific called Oceania. The islands of the South Pacific are grouped with Australia to form Oceania, but they are not actually part of Australia.

For each continent except Antarctica, there is a section on its *terrain*, or land areas; a discussion of its wild animals; a section about what the people who live there do for a living; and an overview of its countries and cities.

Using the Atlas

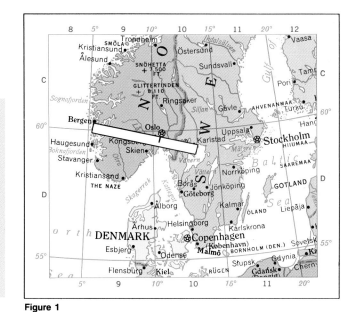

An atlas is a guide to the world that can be used in many ways. But to discover the world with your atlas, you must be able to do five things:

- Measure distances using a map scale.
- Use directions and latitude and longitude.
- Find places on the maps using map keys.
- Use different kinds of maps.
- Use map symbols and legends.

The following sections can help you learn how to do these things.

Figure 1

Measuring Distances

To understand a map, you must know its *scale*, or how large an area of the earth it shows. There are different types of map scales, but the *bar scale* is the easiest to use for finding distance.

For example, to find the distance between Bergen and Oslo in Norway, first you will find out how far Bergen is from Oslo on the map. Then, by using a bar scale, you will learn what this means in actual distance on the earth.

1. Find Bergen and Oslo on the map in Figure 1.
2. Lay a slip of paper on the map so its edge touches the two cities. Move the paper so one corner touches Bergen.
3. Mark the paper where it touches Oslo. The distance from the corner of the paper to the mark shows how far Oslo is from Bergen on the map.
4. The numbers in the map scale in Figure 2 show *statute miles*, or miles on

the earth. Line up the edge of the paper along the map scale, putting the corner at 0.
5. Find the mark on the paper. The mark shows that Bergen is about two hundred miles away from Oslo.

Using Directions and Latitude and Longitude

Most of the maps in this atlas are drawn so north is at the top of the page, south is at the bottom, west is at the left, and east is at the right.

Many of the maps also have lines drawn across them—lines of *latitude* and *longitude*. These are lines drawn on a map or globe to make it easier to tell directions and to locate places.

Latitude lines are also called *parallels*. As shown in Figure 3, lines of latitude run east and west. The equator is a line of latitude, and it runs around the middle of the earth. Other lines of latitude measure how far north or south of the equator a place is. Lines of latitude are numbered in *degrees*,

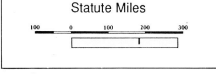

Statute Miles

Figure 2

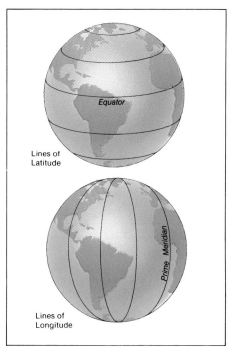

Figure 3

which measure the distance.

The equator is at zero degrees (0°) latitude. The numbers go up in each direction (north and south) the farther you get from the equator. The map in Figure 1 shows that Bergen is north of sixty degrees (60°) latitude and

Stockholm is south of it. So Bergen is farther north than Stockholm.

Lines of longitude run north and south between the two poles, as you can see from Figure 3. Longitude lines are also called *meridians*. Like latitude, longitude is also measured in degrees.

The *prime meridian* is at zero degrees (0°) longitude. Lines of longitude measure how far east or west a place is from the prime meridian. The numbers go up as you travel in each direction (east and west). In Figure 1, Bergen is about five degrees (5°) east of the prime meridian, and Stockholm is about twenty degrees (20°) east. So Stockholm is farther east than Bergen.

Using Map Keys

One of the most important things an atlas can do is tell you the location of a place. To help you find a place quickly and easily on a map, most atlases have an index that includes both the names of places and a guide that is made up of a letter and a number, or a *map key*.

Say you want to find Santiago, a city in Chile, which is in South America. Here's how you would use the map key.

1. Look up the city's name, Santiago, in the back of the atlas. You'll see an entry like the one in Figure 4. The number *88* is the page on which the map is found. The map key *C2* is the letter-number guide to finding Santiago on the map on page 88.

2. Look at Figure 5. It is a piece of the map of southern South America that you will find on page 88.

3. Find the letters *A* through *C* along the left-hand side of the map. Then find the numbers 2 through 4 along the top edge of the map. These numbers and letters are centered between the lines of latitude and longitude on the map.

4. To find Santiago, use the map key *C2*. Place your left index finger on *C* and your right index finger on 2. Move your left finger

across the map and your right finger down the map, staying within the

Figure 5

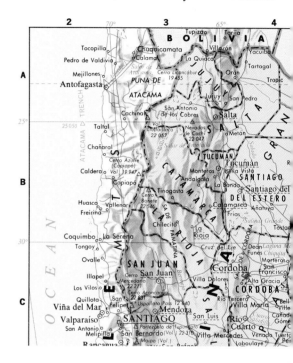

88 South America, South • Physical — Political

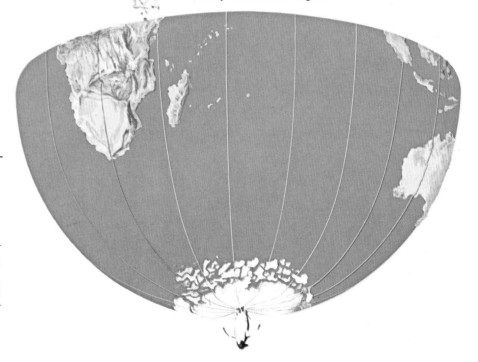

Parallels of latitude are always seventy miles apart. But the distance between meridians shrinks as they approach the North and South poles. At the equator, a giraffe must run seventy miles (112.65 kilometers) to cover one degree of longitude. Near the South Pole, a penguin could easily waddle one degree.

USING THE ATLAS

latitude and longitude lines on either side. Your fingers will meet in the box that contains Santiago.

You can use this method to find any place listed in the index of this atlas. If you see a small, or lowercase, letter in a map key, it refers to the small inset map on the page rather than to the main map on the page. Two map keys are shown for areas that begin on one map and continue on another map.

Using Different Kinds of Maps

There are many different types of maps, and each is especially suited for a certain purpose. For exploring the world's surface, *terrain maps* reveal rugged mountains and continental plains. For special subjects, such as the wildlife of a region, *thematic* maps provide an easy way to see differences throughout the world. For studying countries, *political maps* display the world's nations and cities, roads, and railways. The *physical-political* maps in this atlas tell you the most about each continent. They are the large maps on the pages all by themselves.

The terrain maps go along with the section on the terrain of each continent. These are also called *physical maps* because they show only the physical features of the land. Physical features include oceans, lakes, rivers, glaciers, mountains, and other natural parts of the world.

The thematic maps go with the sections on animals and life on the land. The thematic maps show pictures that tell you about different regions on the map. On the thematic map of the animals of North America, you can see that raccoons live around the Great Lakes. Similar maps throughout the atlas show the kinds of

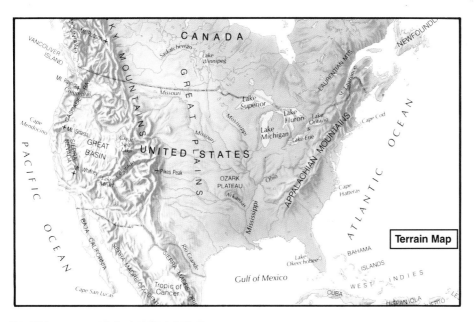

Terrain Map

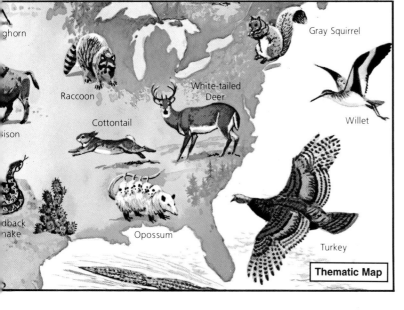

Thematic Map

Political Map

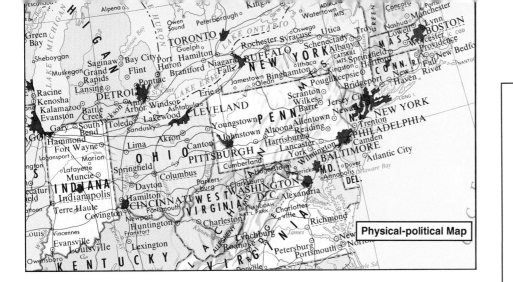

Physical-political Map

wildlife found on each continent. Another type of thematic map shows how people use the land of each continent.

The political maps show the world's political units, the human-made divisions of the earth's surface into countries, states, and cities. These maps go with the sections about countries and cities. They show you the boundaries of each country on the continent as well as the major cities. On the political map of North America, for instance, thick gray lines represent the boundaries of countries. Thinner gray lines show the borders between states or provinces. The thinnest gray lines reveal the locations of railroad tracks; red lines show the major roadways. Other countries, such as Canada and Mexico, are shaded with different colors.

When people think about maps, they usually picture physical-political maps. To get the most information out of these maps, you need to understand what the special symbols on each map represent. You can do that with the help of a *legend,* which is discussed in the next section.

Using Map Symbols and Legends

The easiest way to describe a *symbol* is that it is something that stands for something else. In a way, a whole map is a symbol, because it represents the world or a part of it.

The world's features—such as cities, rivers, and lakes—are represented with symbols on maps. The legend tells you what these symbols mean. On the physical-political maps in this atlas, the symbol for a city might be a dot or a red shaded area, depending on how big the city is. Rivers are shown with blue lines, and railroads are indicated with red lines.

The physical-political map legend at the right divides the earth's geographic features into three major classes: cultural, land, and water features. Cultural features are human-made and include cities, railroads, dams, and political boundaries. Land features are mountain peaks, mountain passes, and *spot heights.* Spot heights tell you the elevation of certain places on a mountain. Water features include rivers, lakes, swamps, and glaciers. Refer to this when working with the physical-political maps.

PHYSICAL-POLITICAL MAP LEGEND

CULTURAL FEATURES

Political Boundaries

- - - - - -	International
━━━━	Intercolonial
- ━ - ━ -	Secondary: State, Provincial, etc.

Cities, Towns and Villages
(Except for scales of 1:20,000,000 or smaller)

PARIS	1,000,000 and over
Ufa	500,000 to 1,000,000
Győr	50,000 to 500,000
Agadir	25,000 to 50,000
Moreno	0 to 25,000
TŌKYŌ	National Capitals
Boise	Secondary Capitals

Transportation

━━━━	Railroads
- - - - -	Railroad Ferries
· · · · · ·	Caravan Routes

Other Cultural Features

	Dams
·━·━·━·	Pipelines
▲	Pyramids
∴	Ruins

LAND FEATURES

△	Peaks, Spot Heights
=	Passes

WATER FEATURES

Lakes and Reservoirs

	Fresh Water
	Fresh Water: Intermittent
	Salt Water
	Salt Water: Intermittent

Other Water Features

	Swamps
	Glaciers
	Rivers
	Canals
Aqueduct	Aqueducts
= = = = = =	Ship Channels
	Falls
	Rapids
	Springs
△	Water Depths
	Sand Bars
	Reefs

Europe

Sixth largest continent

•

Second in population: 694,900,000

•

69 cities with over 1 million population

•

Highest mountain: Elbrus, 18,510 feet
(5,642 meters)

•

Rome and Chicago are the same
latitude

Europe
Terrain

Many parts of Europe lie under the shadows of towering mountains. The most splendid of these peaks are the Alps, which make up a mountain range that winds through Switzerland, southeastern France, Austria, southern Germany, northern Italy, and eastward into Slovenia. Three other mountain ranges spread out from the central mass of the Alps into other countries.

Across the English Channel from mainland Europe are the islands that form the United Kingdom. England lies on the biggest island, and central mountains called the Pennines run through that country like a bumpy backbone.

Northern mainland Europe

© 1992 Rand McNally & Co.

has many mountains. The uplands of Norway and Sweden are bleak and barren. Long ago huge rivers of ice called *glaciers* ground their way across this land, carving deep grooves in between the mountains. The grooves flooded with water from the sea and have become long waterways called *fjords*. Far to the east the Ural Mountains in Russia mark the division between Europe and Asia. To the southwest of the Alps, the Pyrenees separate France and Spain. Spain and Portugal lie on a *peninsula*, a body of land that is almost surrounded by water.

Many famous rivers flow from Europe's mountains. Perhaps the best known, the Rhine, flows north out of Switzerland, past France, and through Germany and the Netherlands. The Danube is another large river that flows through Germany.

The north-central part of Europe is a fertile area known as the Great European Plain. The rich farmlands of this region supply food for much of Europe, and its minerals help to make the Ruhr Valley on the Rhine River a world center for heavy industry.

Many islands lie to the south of mainland Europe in the Mediterranean Sea. They include Corsica, Sardinia, Sicily, and the isles of Greece. The warm, sunny beaches of the Mediterranean are popular with tourists.

County Kerry, in the southwest corner of Ireland, features green pastures and rugged coastlines.

aspian Sea

The rugged, snow capped peaks of the Swiss Alps provide a splendid background for skiers. Tourism is an important part of Switzerland's economy.

Mykonos, shown here, and the other Greek islands in the Aegean Sea are part of the Pindus Mountains. Millions of years ago, a rising sea covered all but the mountain peaks.

EUROPE
Animals

Skua

Herring

Barnacle
Goose

Reindeer

Grey Seal

Wolverine

Lemming

Hare

Red Deer

Basking Shark

Otter

Black
Grouse

Badger

Pheasant

Hedgehog

Atlantic
Salmon

Rabbit

Fox

Moorhen

Chamois

Red-legged
Partridge

Marmot

Squirrel

Stork

Great
Bustard

Barbary Ape

Sole

Ferruginous
Duck

Hoopoe

Spanish Mackerel

Raven

Whimbrel

Brown Bear

Pine Marten

Wild Boar

Wolf

Griffon Vulture

Roe Deer

Lesser Spotted Eagle

Tur

Octopus

Conger Eel

Most of the vast, animal-filled forests that once covered much of Europe were cut down long ago to make room for farms, cities, and towns. Many of Europe's animals were hunted for centuries until they were wiped out. But in the few wild places that remain—mostly national parks and game preserves where animals are protected—some of the animals that once abounded in Europe can still be found.

Shaggy wild boars with curved tusks can be found in the forests of central Europe. Packs of wolves still live in some places, and in northern Russia, the huge brown bear still lumbers about.

Many smaller types of animals live in Europe. Foxes, badgers, moles, rabbits, and squirrels are found in many places. Plump little lemmings abound in the mountains of Norway and Sweden. The hedgehog is common in northern Europe.

Small, striped wildcats prowl in parts of eastern Europe. A rather large wildcat, the Spanish lynx, lives in Spain. Three feet (0.91 meter) long with pointed ears and thick whiskers, the lynx is a fast, fierce hunter.

Sparrows, thrushes, finches, nightingales, and ravens are found throughout central Europe. So are large birds of prey such as falcons and eagles. During the summer, the big white stork is a common sight in cities of the Netherlands, Belgium, and Germany, where it nests on the chimneys of houses.

In a protected forest of Poland about 1,600 *wisents*, bison of prehistoric Europe, feed in grassy clearings just as they did thousands of years ago. They stand up to six feet (1.82 meters) high at the shoulder.

EUROPE
Life on the Land

Fishing

Hydrothermal Plant

Fishing

Offshore Oil Drilling

Fishing

Canneries

Papermaking

Lumbering

Coal Mining

Reindeer Herding

Agricultural Area

Dairyland

Cheese Making

Dairyland

Troika
(3-horse Sleigh)

Agricultural Area

Agricultural Area

Heavy Industry

Houses of Parliament

Bulb Farming

Heavy Industry (Steel)

Grimm's Fairy Tale Country

Farming

Oil Fields

Dairyland

Eiffel Tower

Vineyards

Light Industry

Wheatlands

Citrus Groves

Export by Sea

Matterhorn

Cork Harvesting

Sheep Raised

Water Sports

Roman Ruins

Opera

Olive Orchards

Olive Orchards

Bullfighting

Vineyards

Ancient Greek Ruins

Fishing

Vineyards

Fur Trapping

Lumbering

Oil Fields

Sawmills

Lumbering

Ballet

Oil Fields

St. Basil's

Wheatlands

Agricultural Area

Coal Mining

Agricultural Area

Fishing

Smelting of Ore

Oil Fields

Caviar Exported

Agricultural Area

Fishing

Cotton

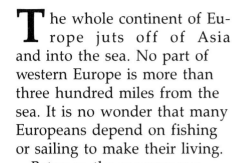

The whole continent of Europe juts off of Asia and into the sea. No part of western Europe is more than three hundred miles from the sea. It is no wonder that many Europeans depend on fishing or sailing to make their living.

Between the many mountains of Europe lie most of Europe's farms. More than half of the land of Europe is used for farming. The raising of livestock is also important throughout Europe.

Modern industry, especially mining and manufacturing, began in Europe. Today, many world industrial leaders are European nations.

Europe's island nations, Iceland, Ireland, and Great Britain, are no less a part of the continent. The United Kingdom unites the four regions known as England, Scotland, Wales (together called Great Britain), and Northern Ireland. Climate limits agriculture, but the use of mechanized farming methods allows the nation to produce half its food supply.

The northern countries of Europe contain fewer people than the rest of the continent. The thick forests provide these countries with an important resource: wood. All three nations export pulp, paper, furniture, and other wood products.

Europe is smaller than any other continent except Australia. But it has more people than any other continent except for Asia. As a result, Europe is very densely populated.

EUROPE
Countries and Cities

Europe has seen many wars, most of them fought over pieces of land. Thus the boundaries of countries have shifted many times over the centuries. In the 1990s, East and West Germany reunited to again form a single Germany.

The republics that were part of the Soviet Union gained independence and Czechoslovakia divided to form the Czech Republic and Slovakia.

Usually, the borders of countries form around natural barriers, such as rivers, seas, or

mountain ranges. The reason for this is that these are places where people can easily defend themselves from attack. Many European nations are edged by such natural borders.

Today, most European countries elect their leaders. In

some countries, the descendants of the kings and queens that ruled most European countries in earlier times are still treated as royalty, but they do not rule the country.

Travelers to Europe must deal with the continent's many languages. Latin-speaking Romans once conquered much of Europe; today the French, Italians, Spanish, Portuguese, and Romanians speak different tongues—the so-called *Romance* languages—that are based on the ancient Latin. The people of Germany, the Netherlands, England, Denmark, Sweden, and Norway speak languages rooted in a single, ancient tongue—the German of the tribes that occupied those areas in ages past. To the east, the peoples of Poland, the Czech Republic, Slovakia, Bulgaria, and other eastern European nations speak languages based on Slavic dialects.

Europe has many big cities that are rich in history and culture. Rome, Italy, and Athens, Greece, were known thousands of years ago. Paris dates back more than two thousand years. It was founded around 52 B.C. by soldiers of the Roman Empire. Trondheim, in Norway, had its beginning around A.D. 998.

The city of Paris and its surrounding area make up the second largest metropolitan area in Europe. The Eiffel Tower, shown here, has become a symbol of French achievement.

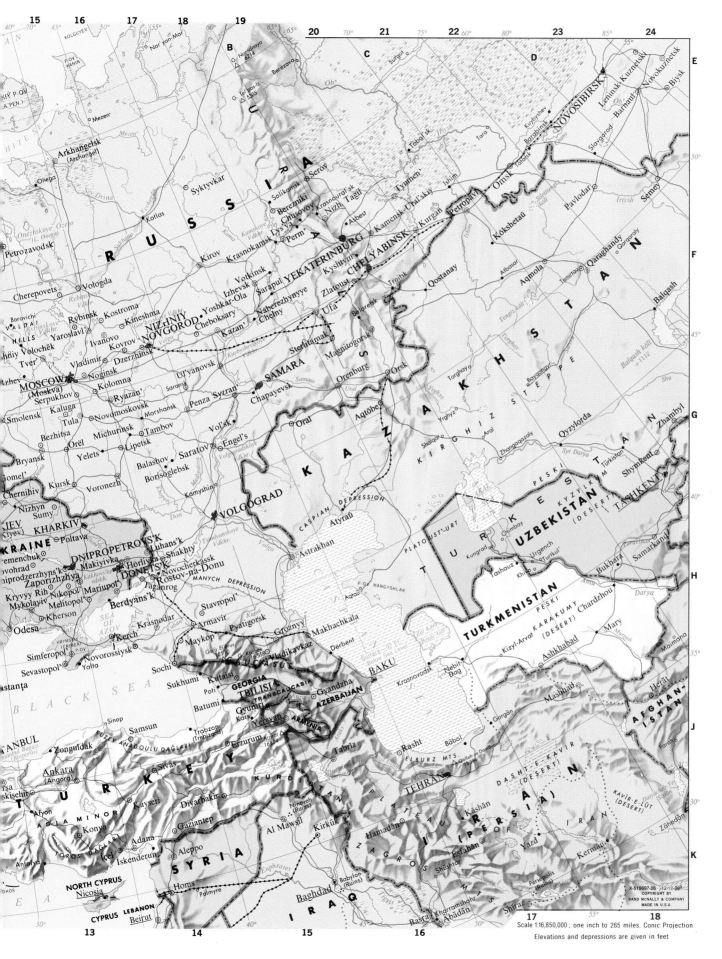

Scale 1:16,850,000 ; one inch to 265 miles. Conic Projection
Elevations and depressions are given in feet

Scale 1:21,500,000; one inch to 340 miles
Lambert's Azimuthal, Equal Area Projection
Elevations and depressions are given in

Asia
Terrain

Asia

Largest continent

•

First in population: 3,337,800,000

•

126 cities with over 1 million population

•

World's highest mountain: Everest, 29,028 feet (8,848 meters)

•

World's largest "lake": Caspian Sea, 143,240 square miles (370,990 square kilometers)

•

World's lowest inland point: Dead Sea, 1,312 feet (400 meters) below sea level

Asia is the largest continent. It covers more area than North America, Europe, and Australia combined. Because it is so big, it is a land of many extremes. It has some of the world's highest mountains, longest rivers, largest deserts, and coldest and hottest climates.

Asia begins at the Ural Mountains in Russia and extends more than three thousand miles (almost five thousand kilometers), all the way to the Pacific Ocean. This northern region is known as Siberia.

To the south of Siberia is an equally large, equally harsh region. This area begins in the deserts of Saudi Arabia and sweeps across central Asia through Iraq, Iran, into Turkmenistan and Kazakhstan, through parts of China, and on into the deserts of Mongolia.

The region is bounded in the south by the highest mountains on the earth: the Himalayas. The mountains thrust up when the Indian subcontinent crashed into Asia millions of years ago. The two peaks that are considered the highest in the world, Mount Everest and K2, are in the Himalayas.

The erosion of limestone created this unusual cone-shaped hill near Guilin in southeastern China. Regions such as these are called *karst*. Images of karst can often be found in traditional Chinese art.

In northern Pakistan, apricots grown in the rugged terrain and harsh climate of the Himalayas dry in the sun. The highest mountains in the world, the Himalayas stretch some 1,550 miles (2,500 kilometers) across central Asia and cut across five countries.

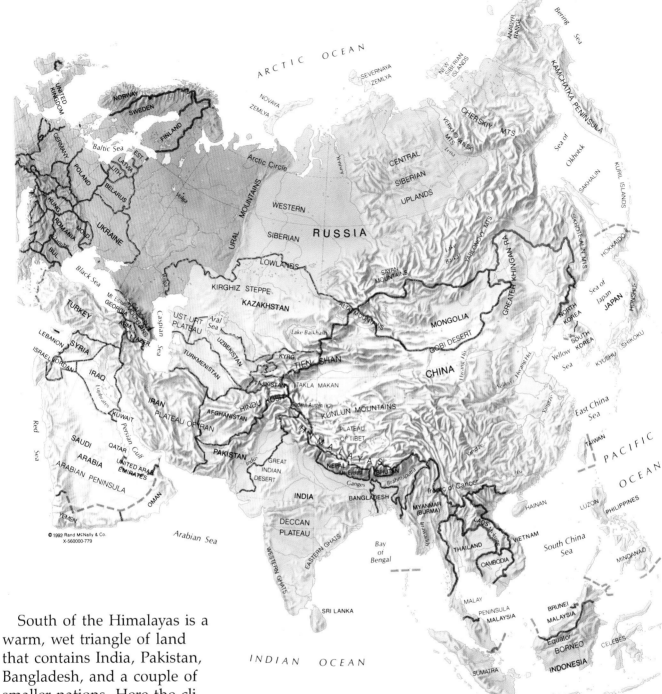

South of the Himalayas is a warm, wet triangle of land that contains India, Pakistan, Bangladesh, and a couple of smaller nations. Here the climate is friendlier and the land more fertile, so many people live in this area. In fact, this is one of the world's most crowded regions.

To the east lies Southeast Asia, a land that is a giant rain forest. It is very fertile and has plenty of rainfall. These factors make Southeast Asia a good place to live, so the countries of this region are highly populated.

North of Southeast Asia is an area known as the Far East. It includes most of China, North Korea, South Korea, and Japan. Many people live in these countries. In fact, China holds more people—over one billion—than any other country in the world.

The four main Japanese islands are part of a chain of recently formed volcanic mountains. Mountains cover two-thirds of the country.

Animals

Asia spreads from far northern lands covered with snow nine months a year to the steamy, hot rain forests that skirt the equator. This wide range of environments provides habitats for an enormous variety of animals.

Large white polar bears leap among the ice floes in the northernmost Siberian coasts. Reindeer, foxes, hares, and tiny, mouselike lemmings live in northern Asia. In northern China and Korea lives the thick-furred Siberian tiger, completely at home in cold and snow.

The forests of southern Asia swarm with animals—monkeys, tree-dwelling leopards, small herds of wild cattle called gaurs, and an ever-dwindling number of tigers. Indian elephants move through the forests in herds numbering from ten to fifty.

The deadly king cobra, the world's longest poisonous snake, also makes the forest its home. Its bite can kill a human within fifteen minutes. The cobra's enemy, the mongoose, also lives in the Asian forests. The fast, clever mongoose will attack and eat a cobra—or any other snake—on sight.

In the high bamboo forests in part of central China lives the giant panda. Mostly white with black legs, ears, and eye patches, this gentle bear-like creature is active mostly at night. The smaller red panda, which looks something like a raccoon, can be found in the Himalayas and the mountains of western China and northern Myanmar (Burma).

Imperial Eagle

Jackal

Dromedary

Jerboa

Ibex

The largest horns grown by any animal are those of a sheep called the Pamir argali, or Marco Polo's argali. Marco Polo found this unusual creature during his travels across central Asia. The sheep's horns spiral outward and have been known to reach seventy-five inches (190.5 centimeters).

Polar Bear

Killer Whale

Arctic Fox

Willow Grouse

Sea Eagle

Wolf

Elk

Snowy Owl

Harbor Seal

Lynx

Przewalski's Horse

Raccoon-like Dog

Japanese Macaque

Saiga

Japanese Crane

Yak

Giant Panda

Bactrian Camel

Mandarin Duck

Snow Leopard

Pheasant

Water Buffalo

Dolphin

Indian Elephant

Cormorant

Flyingfish

Tiger

Peafowl

Gibbon

Macaque

Cobra

Mongoose

Orangutan

ASIA
Life on the Land

More than half the earth's people live on the vast continent of Asia. Throughout the world, people naturally tend to live in areas where the climate and land are good for producing food. About two-thirds of Asia's population make their living by farming, and the continent's agricultural areas are among its most crowded.

In much of China, Japan, India, and the tropical lands of Southeast Asia, the most important crop is rice. It is the main food of many Asian people, and Asia produces most of the world's rice. Cotton is the main crop of parts of southwestern Asia, also known as the Middle East.

The land of northern Asia is too cold for much farming, and the soil in central Asia is not good for growing crops. In these regions, some people raise cattle and sheep.

Petroleum, or crude oil, is a precious substance in today's world. Beneath the deserts of the Middle East lie some of the world's greatest oil reserves. The countries of this region sell, or *export*, oil to many other countries around the world.

There is not much industry in most of Asia, but there is a lot in Israel, China, and western Russia. Industry in South Korea, Taiwan, Singapore, and Hong Kong is growing rapidly. Japan, which has few natural resources, continues to be a leader in world industry, producing automobiles, chemicals, and electronic equipment.

The Arabs of the Middle East tell a story about a young boy named Aladdin, who finds an old lamp. When he rubs the lamp, a genie appears and grants him three wishes.

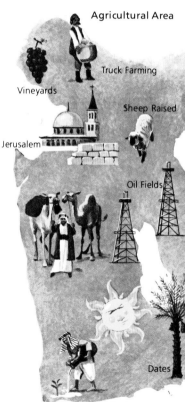

Agricultural Area

Truck Farming

Vineyards

Sheep Raised

Jerusalem

Oil Fields

Dates

Farming by Irrigation

The Indonesian island of Bali, off of Southeast Asia, is known for its folk dances. One, called the *legong*, tells an ancient story of love and battle. Each movement has a meaning and tells a part of the story.

Mining

Fur Trapping

Logging

Truck Farming

Reindeer Herds

Mining

Smelting of Ore

Truck Farming

Logging

Mining

Rice Grown

Cossack Dancer

Wheatlands

Light and Heavy Industry

Wheatlands

Tea Grown

Hydroelectric Power

Great Wall of China

Steel Manufactured

Citrus Fruits Grown

Sheep Raised

Farming

Gate of Heavenly Peace

Chinese Junk

Goods Shipped by Caravan

Smelting of Ore

Traditional Chinese Urn

Agricultural Area

Ruins of Persepolis, Persia

Palace of the Dalai Lama

Cacao (Chocolate)

Agricultural Area

Corn

Manufacturing

Persian Carpet

Wheat

Coconuts

Cotton

Mt. Everest

Bathing in the Sacred Ganges

Taj Mahal

Fishing

Burmese Temples

Logging

Rice Grown

Tea Grown

Oil

Coconuts

Agricultural Area

Rubber

Fishing

Teak

Coffee

ASIA
Countries and Cities

The nations of immense Asia tended to form in clusters. The continent has five large groupings of nations. The first, which borders the eastern edge of the continent, is called the Far East and its leading countries include China and Japan. Indochina and the islands of Indonesia make up the second group, and a third formed within the triangle of land which contains India. The desert countries make up a fourth cluster. Siberia, a part of northern Russia, stands alone as the fifth.

China holds the most people of any nation—over one billion. One out of every five persons on earth is Chinese!

With a history of more than five thousand years, Jerusalem has long been a holy city of Christianity, Judaism, and Islam. The city, divided after one war and reunified in another, was declared Israel's permanent capital in 1980.

EUROPE

Moscow

Yekaterinburg

Istanbul

Ankara

GEORGIA
Tbilisi

ARMENIA
Yerevan

TURKEY

KAZAKHSTAN

Baku

AZERBAIJAN

UZBEKISTAN

Alma-Ata

LEBANON
Beirut

ISRAEL
Jerusalem

SYRIA
Damascus

Amman

JORDAN

IRAQ
Baghdad

Tehran

TURKMENISTAN

Ashkhabad

Tashkent

KYRGYZS

Dushanbe

TAJIKISTAN

IRAN

Kuwait
KUWAIT

Tropic of Cancer

Riyadh

AFGHANISTAN
Kabul

Islamabad

Bishk

SAUDI ARABIA

QATAR
U.A.E.

PAKISTAN

Lahore

New Delhi

Delhi

Muscat

Karachi

Sana

YEMEN

OMAN

INDIA

Aden

© 1992 Rand McNally & Co.
X-560000-279

Ahmadabad

Bombay

Hyderabad

Bangalore

Madras

SRI LA

Colombo

MALDIVES

Roads
Railroads

But in terms of industry, Japan is a giant. The tiny island nation is one of the world's leading industrial powers.

The second cluster of countries occurs in Indochina. Many of the nations of Indochina formed around river valleys where food grows well. Myanmar (Burma) formed around the Irrawaddy River, and Thailand around the Menam. Cambodia and Vietnam share the lower Mekong River, while Laos grew around the northern part.

India, Pakistan, Bangladesh, and Sri Lanka, countries of the third grouping, struggle with poverty. Nearly 874 million people live in India, giving it a population second only to China's. Neighboring Bangladesh has fertile lands, but poor farming methods keep rice in short supply.

The fourth cluster of Asian nations lies on the deserts. Fewer people live here. Turkey, with more farmland than other countries in the region, has just fifty-nine million people. Only in Israel, established in 1948 as a Jewish homeland, does the population density approach that of European countries.

Siberia, the fifth region of Asia, is part of Russia. Its people are few and far between. Much of Russia's coal comes from the industrialized Kuznetsk Basin area, which also produces building materials, chemicals, and machinery.

ATLANTIC OCEAN

ARCTIC OCEAN

North Pole

GREENLAND (Den.)

Meridian of Greenwich

RUSSIA

SIBERIA

KAZAKHSTAN

KIRGHIZ STEPPE

MONGOLIA

CHINA

TURKEY

SYRIA
IRAQ
IRAN
AFGHANISTAN
PAKISTAN

SAUDI ARABIA

YEMEN
OMAN
QATAR
UNITED ARAB EMIRATES
KUWAIT

INDIA

NEPAL
BHUTAN
BANGLADESH
MYANMAR

SRI LANKA (CEYLON)

MALDIVES

INDIAN OCEAN

ARABIAN SEA

BAY OF BENGAL

MEDITERRANEAN SEA

AFRICA

40,000 SQ MI
AREA

0   300   600
Miles

X-519695-26
COPYRIGHT BY
RAND McNALLY & COMPANY
MADE IN U.S.A.

Scale 1:42,000,000; one inch to 665 miles. Lambert's Azimuthal, Equal Area Projection
Elevations and depressions are given in feet

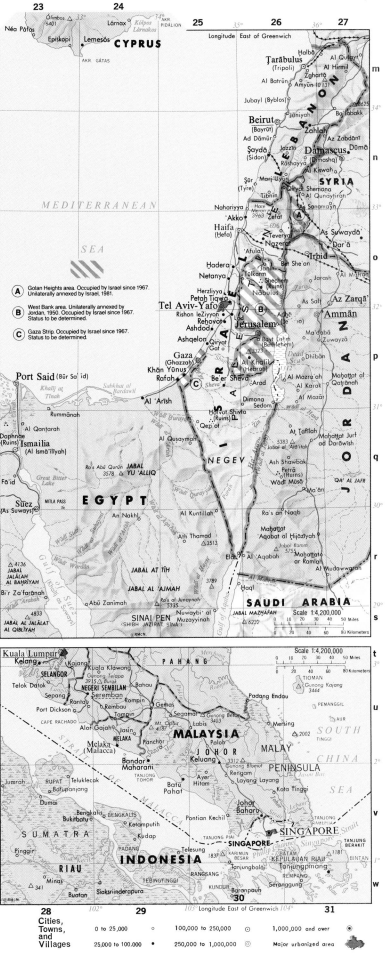

Africa

Second largest continent

•

Third in population: 668,700,000

•

28 cities with over 1 million population

•

Highest mountain: Kilimanjaro, 19,340 feet (5,895 meters)

•

World's largest desert: Sahara, approximately 3,500,000 square miles (9,065,000 square kilometers)

•

World's longest river system: Nile, 4,145 miles (6,671 kilometers)

•

World's highest recorded temperature: Azizia, Libya, 136.4°F (58°C)

•

Equator passes through

Africa
Terrain

The continent of Africa is second in size only to Asia. Yet few people realize just how huge it is. For example, the entire continental United States (which excludes Alaska and Hawaii) could be tucked comfortably into the Sahara Desert, which extends 3,200 miles (5,150 kilometers) across northern Africa.

Many people imagine Africa as a land of rain forests. In reality, most of Africa is covered with desert or grassland. The Sahara takes up most of northern Africa; the Kalahari and Namib deserts lie in the south. Between these two desert regions are many, many miles of grassland called *savanna*. Rain forests, following the equator, mainly occupy the middle of the continent.

Africa has some magnificent mountains, but it lacks the huge chains common to most of the other continents. The Atlas Mountains arch across the top of Africa, through Morocco, Algeria, and Tunisia, forming a barrier between the northern coast and the Sahara. They were raised over thirty million years ago, at the same time as the Alps of Europe.

In East Africa, mountain peaks follow two nearly parallel straight lines. Among the eastern mountains, snow-capped Mount Kilimanjaro, Africa's highest peak, soars to more than nineteen thousand feet.

Shown here is the type of grassland, called savanna, that covers much of Africa. This particular scene is in the nation of Zambia.

Africa's Great Rift Valley extends about four thousand miles (almost 6,500 kilometers). It can be traced along the many lakes and seas that fill parts of it. The cutaway at right shows some of those bodies of water.

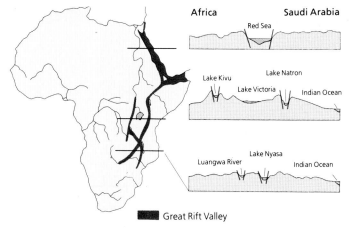

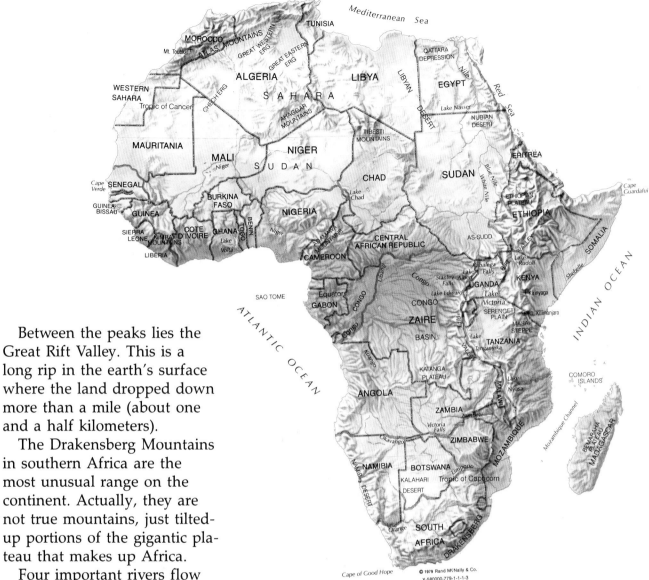

Between the peaks lies the Great Rift Valley. This is a long rip in the earth's surface where the land dropped down more than a mile (about one and a half kilometers).

The Drakensberg Mountains in southern Africa are the most unusual range on the continent. Actually, they are not true mountains, just tilted-up portions of the gigantic plateau that makes up Africa.

Four important rivers flow out of Africa. The Niger runs through several West African countries and out into the Atlantic Ocean. The Congo flows west out of central Africa. The Zambezi, toward southern Africa, flows east to the Indian Ocean. And finally, the great Nile flows northward through several countries, including Egypt, and empties into the Mediterranean Sea. The Nile is the longest river in the world.

Palm trees line the shore along the Gulf of Guinea, which lies to the south of Ghana. This coastal region sports white-sand beaches and blue lagoons.

AFRICA
Animals

Tarpon

Addax

Fennec

Pangolin

Colobus Monkey

Africa is a continent of rain forests, grassy plains, and deserts. Each environment holds different types of animals that have adapted to the conditions. Many African animals are beautiful creatures, but some of these magnificent beasts are in danger of becoming extinct.

In the north the enormous Sahara Desert spreads across thousands of miles. Not many animals can live in that wasteland, and those that do are able to survive with little or no water.

The best-known animal of the Sahara is the one-humped Arabian camel, also known as the dromedary. All camels in the Sahara are used as tame beasts of burden.

The great rain forest of central Africa straddles the equator. Within it roam bands of chimpanzees, which live on fruit and tender plants. The gorilla also lives here, a shy and gentle animal despite its size. Here, too, are found buffalo, leopards, many kinds of monkeys, and the little okapi, a brown-bodied animal with striped legs.

The vast, grassy plains that lie north and south of the central rain forests contain many of the continent's best-known animals. Herds of African elephants, the largest of all land animals, rumble across through the plains. The spotted cheetah, swiftest of all animals, prowls the grasslands in search of prey. It must compete with an even more famous cat, however, for the African lion, a symbol of pride and power, also hunts in the African plains.

Despite their fearsome appearance, gorillas are gentle beasts who eat only plants. Like many African animals, gorillas are threatened with extinction—a result of being hunted and losing their rain forest habitat.

Jackal

Dromedary

Crowned Crane

Eared Vulture

Dorcas Gazelle

Barbary Sheep

Striped Hyena

Crocodile

Greater Kudu

Aardvark

Elephant

Giraffe

Baboon

Chimpanzee

Gorilla

Black Rhinoceros

Leopard

Hornbill

Cape Buffalo

Hippopotamus

White Pelican

Zebra

Lion

Tenrec

Eland

Chameleon

Python

Wildebeest

Ring-tailed Lemur

Cheetah

Impala

Angelfish

Ostrich

Sacred Ibis

AFRICA
Life on the Land

Some Africans carve ceremonial masks by hand, as they have for centuries. This mask is too heavy to wear and is used as a decoration.

Agricultural Area

Peanuts

Chocolate

Most Africans are either farmers or herders. Many of them live as their ancestors did for thousands of years. They roam the land for food or live in tiny villages, raising crops and animals mostly for their own use and not for sale to other countries.

Little farming can be done in hot, dry North Africa. But along the coasts of Morocco, Algeria, and Tunisia, farmers can grow a few crops—such as citrus fruits, grapes, almonds, grains, and olives.

Drilling for oil is important to several African countries. Algeria and Libya in the north and the nations of Nigeria and Gabon farther south export oil and natural gas to other countries.

West Africa is an important agricultural area. Among other crops, people here grow cacao beans, from which chocolate and cocoa are made. The forests of central Africa produce rubber trees and banana trees. In East Africa, herding cattle has been the main way of life for many years.

Farther south, in the country of South Africa, the fertile land is farmed by the descendants of Europeans who settled there many years ago. The land of South Africa also holds many minerals, such as platinum, antimony, chromium, and manganese. Most of the world's diamonds—both gems and those used in industry—and much of its gold come from South African mines. This vast mineral wealth helped build South Africa into the continent's most industrialized nation.

Ananse the Spider Man is a character in a famous African tale. Ananse gathered all the wisdom in the world into a huge pot and tried to keep it for himself. But the pot fell as Ananse tried to hide it in a tree, and all the wisdom blew away.

Agricultural Area

Moorish-style Architecture

Corn

Wheat

Vineyards

Olives

Fishing

Cairo

Tobacco

Sphinx

Nomad with Goats

Oil Fields

Dates Harvested

Goods Shipped by Caravan

The Great Pyramid
at Giza

Sand Dunes

Cotton Grown

Cotton Made into Cloth

African Village

Leather Products Made

Cattle Raised

Sheep Raised

Rubber

Palm Oil

Mining

Plantains (African Bananas)

Tourists
Welcomed

Cattle Raised

Cacao Beans (Chocolate)

Central Forests

Copra (Dried Coconut) Shipped

Oil Fields

Pygmy

Mt. Kilimanjaro

Minerals Mined

Agricultural Area

Masai
Tribesman

Corn

Coal Mines

Tea

Victoria Falls

Diamond Mines

Citrus Fruits

Sheep Raised

Yams

Vanilla Beans Grown

Gold Mines

AFRICA
Countries and Cities

Human history began in Africa. Scientists believe that the earliest human beings walked the grasslands of East Africa about two million years ago. Over many years, humans migrated out of Africa to inhabit other parts of the world.

Civilization has a long history in North Africa. The Nile Valley of Egypt cradled the center of one of the world's oldest civilizations, which developed over five thousand years ago. Some of the cities of Egypt, including Alexandria and Cairo, are more than one thousand years old. Cairo is

—— Roads
—— Railroads

Algiers Tunis
Casablanca Rabat TUNISIA Tripoli
MOROCCO Alexandria
  Cairo
ALGERIA LIBYA EGYPT
WESTERN SAHARA Aswan
Tropic of Cancer
Nouakchott MAURITANIA
CAPE VERDE MALI NIGER ERITREA
Dakar SENEGAL Khartoum Asmera
GAMBIA Bamako CHAD SUDAN DJIBOUTI
GUINEA-BISSAU BURKINA FASO N'Djamena
GUINEA Niamey
Conakry BENIN ETHIOPIA
Freetown COTE GHANA TOGO NIGERIA Addis Ababa
SIERRA LEONE D'IVOIRE
LIBERIA Accra Lagos CENTRAL AFRICAN REPUBLIC SOMALIA
Abidjan CAMEROON
EQUATORIAL GUINEA Yaounde UGANDA Mogadishu
SAO TOME AND PRINCIPE KENYA
Libreville Equator Kampala
GABON CONGO Nairobi
RWANDA
Brazzaville ZAIRE BURUNDI Mombasa
CABINDA Kinshasa
(ANG.) TANZANIA
Luanda Dar es Salaam
COMOROS
ANGOLA MALAWI
ZAMBIA
Lusaka
Harare
ZIMBABWE MOZAMBIQUE
NAMIBIA Antananarivo
Windhoek BOTSWANA MADAGASCAR
Walvis Bay Tropic of Capricorn
(S. AFRICA)
Gaborone Pretoria
Johannesburg SWAZ. Maputo
LESOTHO Durban
SOUTH
AFRICA
Cape Town
© 1979 Rand McNally & Co.
X-580000-279-2-2-3

Country borders mean little to independent nomads like the Masai people. They cross the boundary between Kenya and Tanzania often in search of water and grazing lands for their cattle.

Tunisia's population is concentrated along the coast, but village scenes such as this one are common in the nation's semi-arid mountain regions. Most of the inhabitants of these central and southern areas live in houses of stone and mud.

In many African nations, the capital city is the only sizable urban center. Harare, pictured here, is the capital and largest city of Zimbabwe, in southern Africa.

also the biggest city in Africa.

During the seventh century A.D., the religion of Islam was adopted throughout much of North Africa. Beautiful Muslim mosques were built in what is now Libya, Algeria, Tunisia, and Morocco.

By the 1400s, Europeans began sailing to Africa and conquering the peoples who lived there. The Europeans were interested mainly in profiting from the vast resources they found in Africa. By the early 1900s, almost all of Africa was under European rule. The borders of many African countries were set up by European colonists who settled there. Most of the European governments are gone now, replaced by the independent nations.

Much of West Africa is a hot, moist, lowland area. In past centuries raiders visited these shores, kidnaped people, carried them away in ships, and sold them as laborers throughout the world. Today, more than one-fourth of the people in Africa live in these western nations. Nigeria, with over 91 million people, is Africa's most populous country.

The equator passes through central Africa. Steamy Zaire, covered with rain forest, is the biggest country in the region, holding thirty-five million people.

Mountains and the Great Rift Valley separate East Africa from the rest of the continent. Here are grasslands on which groups of people herd cattle and many wild animals roam. Kenya and Tanzania have set aside vast areas where the animals are protected.

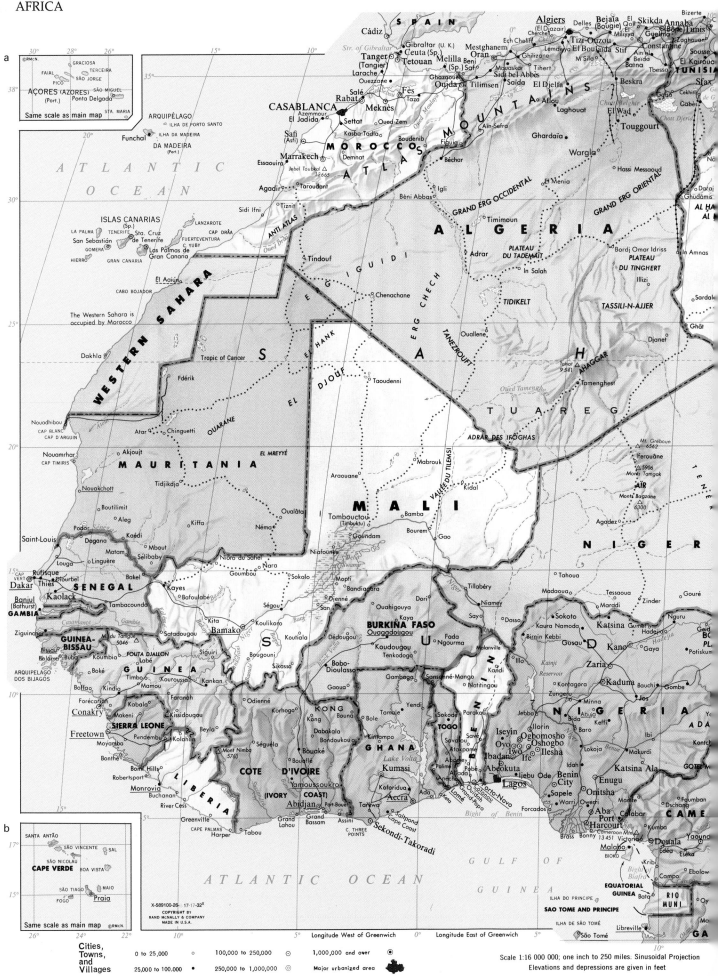

Cities,
Towns,
and
Villages

| 0 to 25,000 | 100,000 to 250,000 ⊙ | 1,000,000 and over ⊚ |
| 25,000 to 100,000 • | 250,000 to 1,000,000 ⊚ | Major urbanized area |

Scale 1:16 000 000; one inch to 250 miles. Sinusoidal Projection
Elevations and depressions are given in feet

X-589100-26 17-17-32X
COPYRIGHT BY
RAND McNALLY & COMPANY
MADE IN U.S.A.

Longitude West of Greenwich   Longitude East of Greenwich

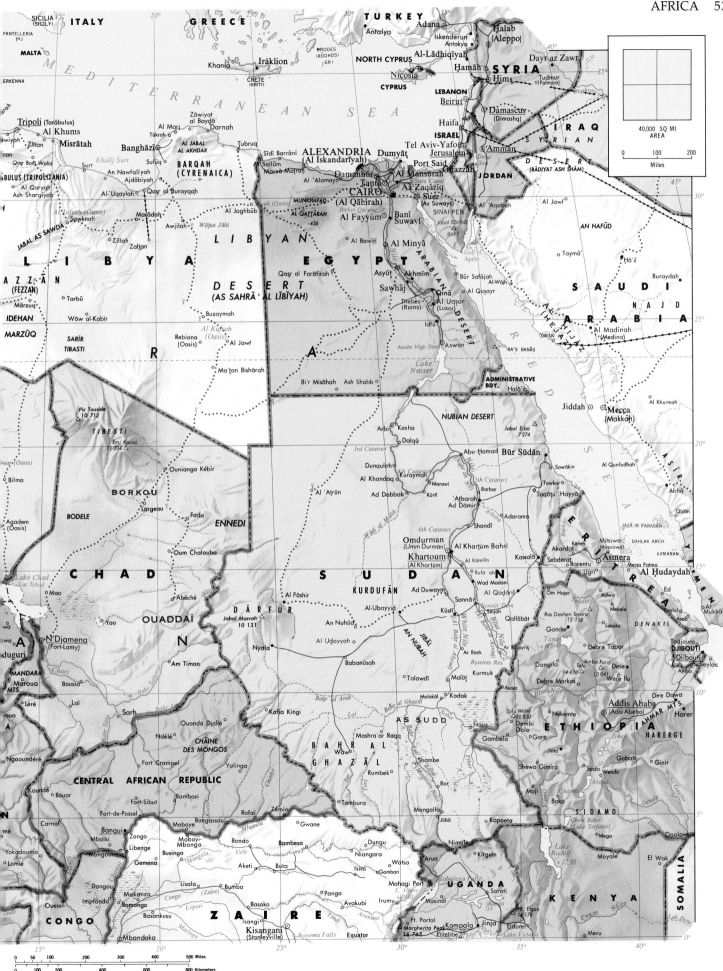

GABON

Libreville
Kango
Ndjolé
Port Gentil
Lambaréné
Lastoursville
Equator
Moanda
Franceville
Sette Cama
Tchibanga
Mbigou
Mayumba

CONGO

Sibiti
Brazzaville
Pointe-Noire
CABINDA
Lândana (Angola)
Cabinda
Soyo
Nóqui
Boma
Matadi
M'banza Congo
Bembe
N'zeto
Uíge
Ambriz
Caxito

Irébou
Owando
Lukoléla
Bolobo
Bandundu
Tshela
Mbanza-Ngungu
Popokabaka
Kikwit
Maquela do Zombo
Cuango
Damba

ZAIRE

Mbandaka
Bikoro
Boende
Itoko
Monkoto
Inongo
Lac Maï-Ndombe (Lake Leopold II) +1076
Lusanga
Kole
Lukenie
Ilebo
Bulungu
Luebo
Djokupunda
Tshikapa

Ubundu
Kindu
Kongolo
Kasongo
Kabalo
Kabambare
Kigoma
Ujiji
Kamina
Kabinda
Kanda Kanda
Mutombo Mukulu

UGANDA
Ripon Falls
Jinja
Entebbe
Kampala
Kisumu
Rutshuru
Gisenyi
RWANDA
Kigali
Astrida
Bukavu
BURUNDI
Gitega
Bujumbura
Uvira
Bukoba
Shirati
Ikoma
Mwanza
Biharamulo
Shinyanga
Kondoa

TANZAN

Kilimatinde
Dodoma
Kasanga
Mbala
Tukuyu
Mwaya
Karonga
Sangea
Kipembawe
Iring
Mporokoso
Kasama
Mbeya
Chinteche
Metangula
Nkhota Kota

ANGOLA

Luanda
Golungo Alto
Catete
Dondo
Kalandula
Malanje
Saurimo
Porto Amboim
Sumbe
Waku Kundo
Lobito
Benguela
Chinguar
Kuito
Munhango
Huambo
Caconda
Dongo
Cuchi
Namibe
Tombua
Cahama
Cassinga
Dima
Humbe
Xangongo
SERRA DA CHELA
PENÍNSULA DOS TIGRES
CAPE FRIA

Kolwezi
Tenke
Kambove
Likasi
Lubumbashi (Elisabethville)
Sakania
Chingola
Ndola
ZAMBIA
Lusaka
Mongu
Kafue
Mazabuka
Pemba
BAROTSELAND
Kalomo
Livingstone
Lake Kariba
Cabora Bassa Res.
Zumbo
Tete
Chiromo
Blanty
Zomba

KATANGA
Kamina
Bukama
Sandoa
Kongolo
Moba
Karema
Pweto
Lake Mweru +3055
Kasenga
Lake Bangweulu +3764
Mansa
Serenje
Chipata
Mchinji
Lilongwe
Mongoche

Kabinda
Kamin
Koni
Panda
Kiambi

MALAWI
Mzimba
Chitipa

RHODESIA
Harare (Salisbury)
Chitungwiza
Chinhoyi
Shamva
Kadoma
Chegutu
Kwekwe
Gweru
Mutare (Umtali)
Chivhu (Enkeldoorn)
Shurugwi
Mandidzudzure
Masvingo
Bulawayo
Zvishavane
ZIMBABWE

Vila de Manica
Dondo
Beira
Nova Mambe
Vilanculos
ILHA DO BAZARUTO
Massinga
Inhambane
Xai-Xai
Manjacaze
Inharrime
Maputo (Lourenço Marques)

CAPRIVI STRIP
Livingstone
Victoria Falls
Hwange

OWAMBO
Ruacana Falls
Namutoni
Etoshapan
Tsumeb
Otavi
Grootfontein
NAMIB
Brandberg 8550
Omaruru
Karibib
Okahandja
NAMIBIA
Outjo
Otjiwarongo
DAMARALAND
Usakos
Swakopmund
Walvis Bay (S. Africa)
Windhoek
Gobabis
Rehoboth

BOTSWANA
Ghanzi
Lake Xau
Maun
Ntwetwe Pan
Okavango Swamp
Makgadikgadi Pans
Francistown
Old Tate
Serowe
Palapye
Mochudi
Gaborone
Molepolole
Lobatse
Mmabatho
Tshabong

KALAHARI DESERT
Ngami

Tuli
Messina
VENDA
Louis Trichardt
Thohoyandou
KRUGER
Pietersburg
Potgietersrus
Nylstroom
TRANSVAAL
BOPHUTHATSWANA
Pretoria
Krugersdorp
JOHANNESBURG
Benoni
Germiston
Standerton
Lydenburg
Barberton
Carolina
Komatipoort
SWAZI-LAND
Mbabane
Piet Retief

GREAT NAMALAND
Maltahöhe
Gibeon
Keetmanshoop
Bethanien
Lüderitz
Aroab

BUSHMANLAND
Warmbad
Oranjemund
Port Nolloth
Springbok
Calvinia
Mateking
Vryburg
Taung
Potchefstroom
Kroonstad
Welkom
ORANGE FREE STATE
Kimberley
Bloemfontein
Hopetown
Kuruman
Upington
Prieska

Wakkerstroom
Ubombo
Vryheid
Nongoma
KWAZULU
Ladysmith
NATAL
Pietermaritzburg
Durban
Port Shepstone
Scottburgh

LESOTHO
Maseru
DRAKENSBERG
Mt. aux Sources 10 822
10 436

SOUTH AFRICA
Springfontein
Britstown
De Aar
Carnarvon
Victoria West
Middelburg
Aliwal North
Maclear
Umtata
TRANSKEI
Port St. Johns
Beaufort West
Graaff Reinet
Cradock
Queenstown
CISKEI
Bisho
King William's Town
East London
Calvinia
Sutherland
GREAT KARROO
Oudtshoorn
Uitenhage
Port Alfred (Kowie)
LITTLE KARROO
Worcester
Paarl
Mosselbaai
Humansdorp
Port Elizabeth
Swellendam
Bredasdorp
CAPE OF GOOD HOPE
CAPE AGULHAS
Malmesbury
Saldanha
St. Helenabaai
Cape Town

The "Homelands" (Bophuthatswana, Ciskei, Transkei, Venda) were unilaterally created by South Africa and are not internationally recognized.

1 Bophuthatswana
2 Ciskei
3 Transkei
4 Venda

X-589200-26   -13V-11V-29¹
COPYRIGHT BY
RAND McNALLY & COMPANY
MADE IN U.S.A.
Tropic of Capricorn

Inset map:

a
ROBBENEILAND
Bloubergstrand
Kanonkop 1502
Milnerton
Durbanville
CAPE TOWN
MOUILLE PT.
Camps Bay
Parow
Bellville
Table Bay
Goodwood
Pinelands
Table Mt. 3567
Nuweland
Kuilsrivier
Wynberg
Ottery
CAPE FLATS
Houtbaai 3048
Chapman's Bay
Muizenberg
SEAL ISLAND
Kommetjie
Grootkop 1286
Simonstad
Vishoek
Valsbaai (False Bay)
Swartkop 2229
SMITSWINKEL VLAKTE
KAAPPUNT
CAPE OF GOOD HOPE

CAPE TOWN
Scale 1:1 000 000
0   5   10 Miles
0   4   8   12   16 Kilometers
®RMCN.

18°30'
15° Longitude East of Greenwich   20°

Scale 1:16 000 000; one inch to 250 miles. Sinusoidal Projection
Elevations and depressions are given in feet

0   50 100   200   300   400   500 Miles
0   100   200   400   600   800 Kilometers

ATLANTIC OCEAN

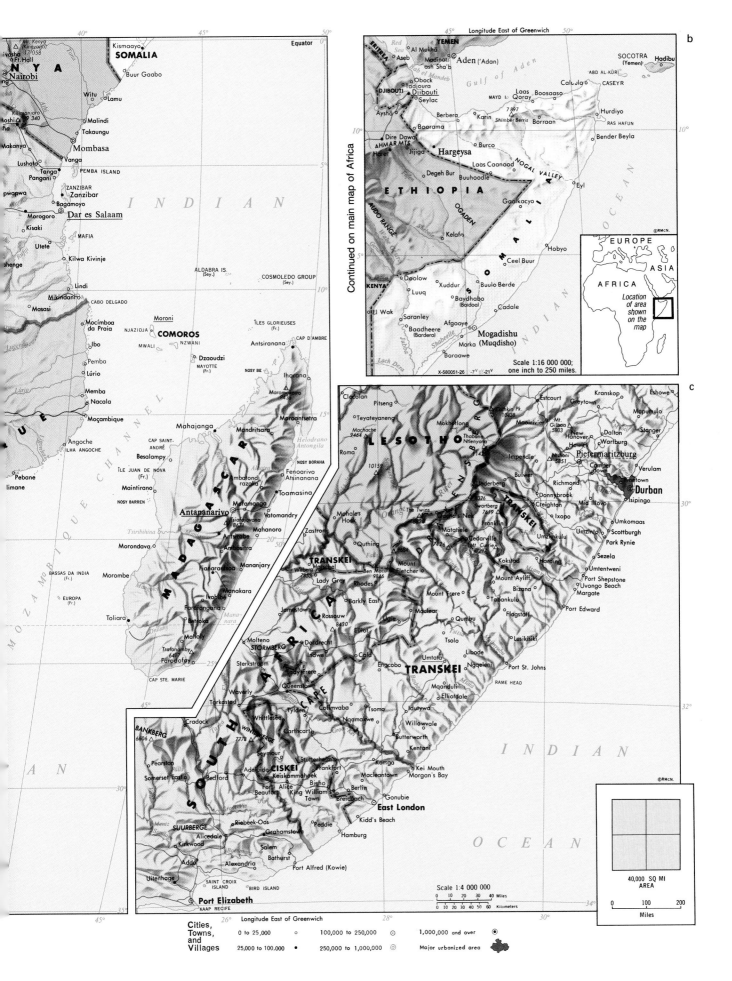

Oceania
Terrain

Deep in the heart of Australia, on the western plateau, lies Mount Olga. A worn-down collection of sandstone blocks, "the Olgas" and nearby Ayers Rock tower above the desert landscape.

A map of the world shows you just how big the Pacific Ocean is. It covers more than one-third of the earth's surface. You can also see that the ocean is full of islands of different sizes. Australia, New Zealand, and other islands in this region known as Oceania lie within the vast Pacific like stepping stones across a pond. Geographers group the islands into three regions. Polynesia includes Hawaii, Samoa, Tahiti, and Easter Island. Micronesia contains the Marshall, Caroline, and Gilbert islands. Melanesia includes the Fiji Islands and New Guinea.

Australia is the smallest continent. The Great Dividing Range thrusts its mountains along the eastern coast. In the south, it dips into the sea and rises up again to form Tasmania. Hammered by wind and water over hundreds of millions of years, the hump-shaped mountains of the Great Dividing Range are truly ancient.

West of the Great Dividing Range is the continent's great desert region. Australians call it the Outback. The mountains keep clouds and rain from moving into the Outback. Part of the Outback is bush country, where some trees and plants grow. The rest is made up of three deserts: the Great Sandy, the Gibson, and the Great Victoria.

The Cape York Peninsula is very different from the rest of Australia. Heat and rain combine to make ideal conditions for the tropical rain forests that grow there.

Perhaps the most famous region of Australia is not on the land, but in the ocean off the

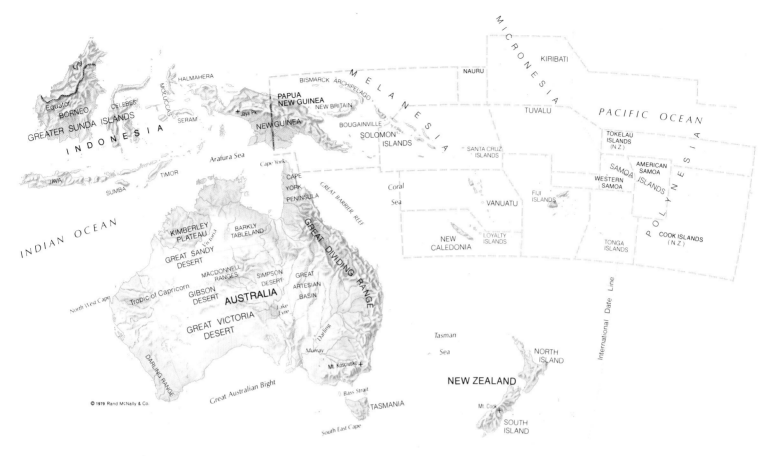

northeastern coast. It is called the Great Barrier Reef. Built from colorful coral formations, it is the largest coral reef in the world and supports a great variety of ocean life.

Two main islands make up New Zealand: North Island and South Island. On the southwest coast of South Island, long, beautiful fjords cut into the land, just like the fjords of Norway. North Island boasts a volcanic region around Lake Taupo.

The Isle of Pines is one of several islands that make up New Caledonia. The culture and pleasant climate of this French territory attract many tourists.

OCEANIA
Animals

Many of the animals of Australia are very different from those in other places. Australia was separated from all other parts of the world for about fifty million years, so its animals evolved in different ways, creating different solutions to the problems of survival. Most Australian *mammals*—furry, warm-blooded animals—are marsupials. Marsupials are animals like the kangaroo whose babies are kept in a pouch on the mother's body until they are old enough to care for themselves.

On the plains of Australia, several kinds of marsupials make their homes. Kangaroos live in little herds and eat grass. Some kangaroos can be as much as seven feet (over two meters) tall, but there are also small kangaroos called wallabies. Wombats look like beavers without tails. They dig tunnels that they sleep in during the day, and then forage for food at night. Ratlike, long-snouted bandicoots live much the same way as wombats.

Dingoes also roam the dry plains of Australia. When the first European settlers arrived, the dingo was the only large, meat-eating mammal on the continent. A member of the dog family, the dingo has long legs, a wolflike head, and yellow-red fur.

In the eastern part of Australia lives the koala. Koalas look like little bears, but in fact they are not. Unlike bears, which are mammals, koalas are marsupials and carry their young in pouches.

New Zealand does not have many animals that have not been brought by people. But on some islands near New Zealand live little reptiles called tuataras. They are the last survivors of a group of reptiles that lived about 225 million years ago—long before the rise of the dinosaurs.

Great numbers of sea creatures drift gracefully among the coral reefs and the deeper tropical waters surrounding the islands of Oceania. Most are brilliantly colored and very beautiful.

Blue Angelfish

Pacific Sheepshead

Albacore

Ocean Sunfish

Eagle Ray

Regal Angelfish

Imperial Angelfish

Sea Horse

Viperfish

Opah

Black Marlin

Triggerfish

Butterfly Fish

Emu

Frilled Lizard

Dingo

Cockatoo

Death Adder

Echidna

Cassowary

Tree Kangaroo

Great Gray Kangaroo

Rabbit

Rock Wallaby

Womba

Koala

Kookaburra

Red Kangaroo

Platypus

Wandering Albatross

White Shark

Slender-billed Shearwater

Black Swan

The koala looks like a soft, cuddly teddy bear. Small, it weighs less than eighteen pounds (8.16 kilograms) when grown. For six months the cub rides in its mother's pouch. Later it rides on her back, even when she climbs high into the eucalyptus trees for the buds and leaves that are the koala's only food.

Dovey Petrel

Kiwi

Tuatara

Kea

OCEANIA
Life on the Land

Lumbering

Rain Forest

Water Sports

Sheep Raising

Lumbering

Water Conservation

Great Barrier Reef

Uranium Prospecting

Aborigines in the Outback

Cattle Raising

Agricultural Area

Mining

Sheep Raising

Ayers Rock

Rugby

Going to School by Radio

Mining

Opals Mined

Sydney—Opera House

Lifeguard Teams

Citrus Groves

Minerals Mined

Agricultural Area

Agricultural Area

Wheatlands

Water Sports

Freighter

Fishing

Fruit Grown

Minerals Exported

Maori Carving

Sheep Raising

During the Age of Discovery, Europeans traveled to Australia, New Zealand, and other islands of Oceania. They settled the lands they found, and many descendants of Europeans remain on those lands.

Australia may be the smallest continent, but it is also one of the largest countries. Its population clings mostly to the coasts along the fertile lands of the east and southeast. Some people live at the edge of the Outback. They are mostly farmers who raise sheep and cattle. Australia's major exports include grain and wool. Today, Australia is highly industrialized.

New Zealand is not as industrialized as Australia, but manufacturing areas such as the paper industry are growing. The mild climate and excellent grazing land makes the raising of sheep and cattle very important in New Zealand.

Countries and Cities

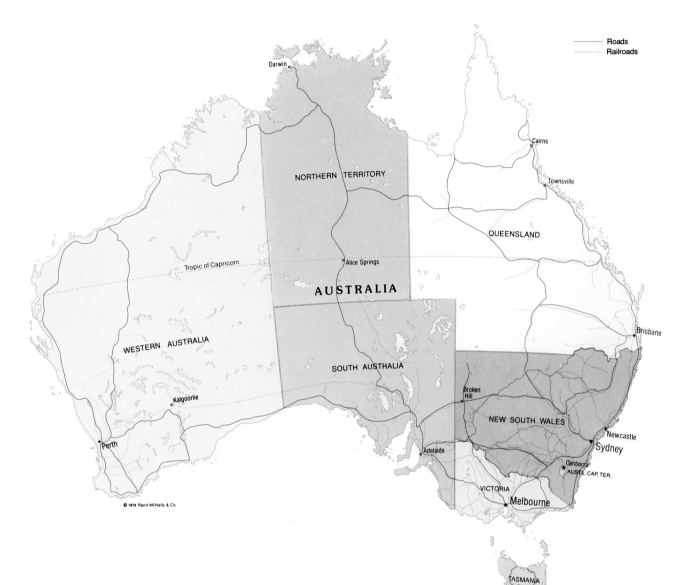

The Land Down Under—that's what Australia and New Zealand are often called. The nickname grew out of the idea that these lands are directly opposite, that is, under the feet of, Europeans.

Australia is divided into states, and its people elect their leaders. New Zealand, also once a British colony, now operates in much the same way.

The islands of Oceania were once colonies, too, but have become nations. Western Samoa, Nauru, Fiji, the Solomon Islands, and the eastern half of New Guinea are now independent.

The descendants of Europeans who live in Australia and New Zealand speak English. There are groups of people in these places and on the surrounding islands who have lived there since ancient times, and most of them speak English, as well as the languages of their ancestors.

2 115° **3** 120° **4** 125° **5** 130° **6** 135° **7**

INDONESIA

Pasuruan
G. Mahameru 12 060
Singaraja Batu
Ratjo
LOMBOK Sumbawa Besar Bima
SUMBAWA FLORES
SUMBA Waingapu
SAWU
ROTI Kupang
ALOR
LOMBLEN PANTAR Dili
SUNDA ISLANDS
TIMOR

SELARU

TANJUNG VALS

A

SUNDA Singaraja

ARAFURA SEA

SUNDA TRENCH

SAVU SEA

TIMOR SEA

C. VAN DIEMEN CROKER
COBURG PEN.
BATHURST MELVILLE
Van Diemen Gulf
Clarence Str.
Darwin
Daly
Anson Bay
Joseph
Bonaparte Gulf
Queens Chan.

WESSEL IS.
CAPE ARNHEM
Blue Mud Bay
GROOTE
EYLANDT
Limmen
Bight
SIR EDWARD PELLEW
GROUP

GULF OF
CARPENTAR

B

INDIAN

CAPE
LONDONDERRY

ARNHEM LAND
Pine Creek
Katherine

Roper

WELLESLEY

Wyndham

BUCCANEER ARCH.
CAPE LEVEQUE
Mt. Hann 2800
KING LEOPOLD RANGES
GEIKIE RANGE
DAMPIER Derby Fitzroy Crossing Halls Creek
Broome LAND
Roebuck Bay
LaGrange

Collier Bay

King Sd.

Fitzroy

Sturt Cr.

Birdum
Victoria River
Downs
Daly Waters
Newcastle Waters

NORTHERN

Tanami Tennant Creek

Borroloola

BARKLY TABLELAND

Alexandria

Burketown

Dobby
Camooweal
Mount Isa
Dajarra

C

OCEAN

LARREY POINT EIGHTY MILE BEACH

Snowy Cr.

RIPON
DAMPIER Port Hedland
ARCHI.
MONTE BELLO IS.
BARROW
Roebourne Marble Bar
Nullagine
NORTH WEST CAPE
Millstream HAMERSLEY RANGE
Onslow Mt. Bruce 4024
Ashburton

DeGrey

Fortescue

GREAT SANDY DESERT
Mackay
Jiggalong
Disappointment
Macdonald

TERRITORY
Barrow Creek

Mt. Ziel 4955
MACDONNELL RANGES Arltunga
Alice Springs
JAMES RANGE
Amadeus
SIMPSON
DESERT

QU

QU

Exmouth Gulf

D

POINT CLOATES
Tropic of Capricorn
CAPE FARQUHAR

Geographe Chan.

CAPE NATURALISTE
Carnarvon
BERNIER Gascoyne
DORRE Shark Bay
DIRK HARTOG
STEEP POINT

WESTERN

GIBSON DESERT

Peak Hill
Nabberu
Carnegie
Wells
Gillen

Charlotte
Waters
MUSGRAVE RANGES
Mt. Woodroffe 4970
EVERARD RANGES
The Alberga

Birdsville

Oodnadatta

A

E

HOUTMAN ROCKS
Geraldton
Mingenew
Dongara

Ajana
Northampton
AUSTRALIA

Meekatharra
Nannine
Cue
Sandstone
Mount Magnet
Austin
Ballard

Wiluna

Yeo

Laverton
Carey
GREAT VICTORIA DESERT

Moore Barlee
Menzies
Pithra
Milling Lake Brown
Moora
SWANLAND
Northam
Southern Cross
Coolgardie Boulder
Kalgoorlie Leonora
Cowan
Dundas
Norseman

Goddards Soak
Rawlinna
Eyre
Eucla

STUART RANGE
William Creek
Marree
Farina

NULLARBOR PLAIN

Ooldea Station

SOUTH AUSTRALIA

FLINDERS RANGES
Everard

Hughes
Penong
POINT FOWLER
Ceduna

Woomera
Parachilna
Pimba
Gairdner
Whyalla Port Augusta
Port Pirie
EYRE PENINSULA
Moonta
Wallaroo

FLIN

Marree
Farina

Peterb
Gladstone

F

Perth
Fremantle
DARLING RANGE
York
Narrogin
Collie
Bunbury
CAPE NATURALISTE Busselton
Katanning
CAPE LEEUWIN Nornalup Albany
PT. D'ENTRECASTEAUX WEST CAPE HOWE
King George Sd.

Salmon Gums
Ravensthorpe
Hopetoun
Esperance
ARCHIPELAGO
OF THE RECHERCHE

GREAT AUSTRALIAN BIGHT

Port Lincoln
KANGAROO

Gulf St. V.
Gawle
Port Wak
Ade

Nar
Kingsto
CAPE JAFFA

Mt. G

Geographe Bay

G

INDIAN

OCEAN

40,000 SQ MI
AREA

0   100   200
Miles

35°

40°

H
110° 1   2   Longitude 115° East of Greenwich 120° 4   125° 5   130° 6   135° 7

A-590200-26- -4-5-13
COPYRIGHT BY
RAND McNALLY & COMPANY
MADE IN U.S.A.

Longitude East of Greenwich

**Cities
and
Towns**
0 to 50,000 ○ 500,000 to 1,000,000 ◎
50,000 to 500,000 ⊙ 1,000,000 and over

Scale 1:16,850,000 ; one inch to 265 miles. Lambert's Azimuthal, Equal Area Projection
Elevations and depressions are given in feet

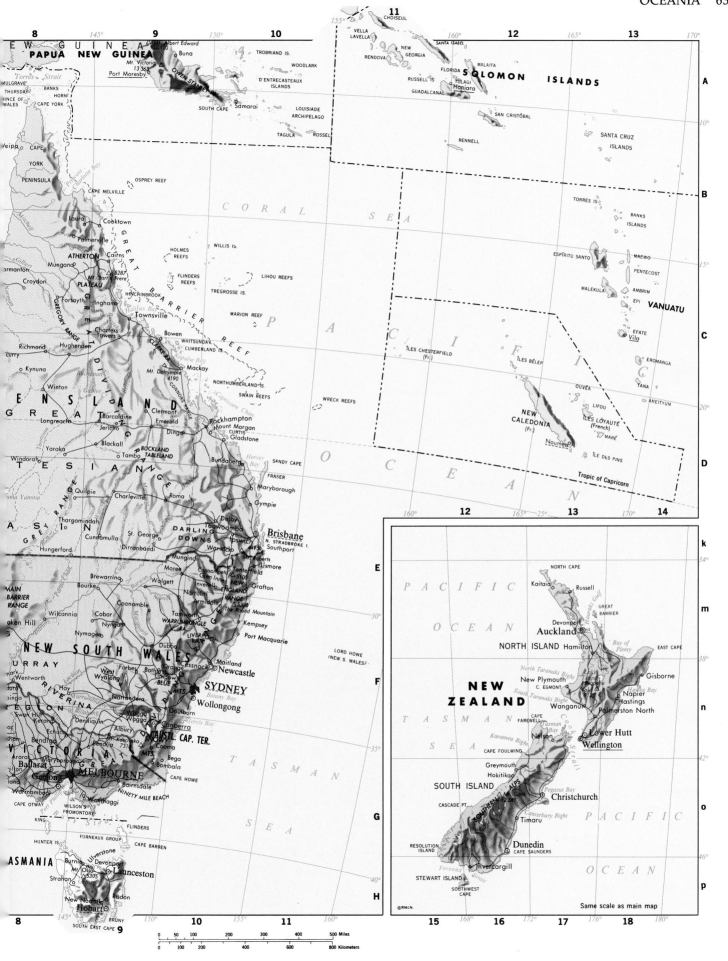

North America

Third largest continent

•

Fourth in population: 438,200,000

•

49 cities with over 1 million population

•

Highest mountain: McKinley, 20,320 feet (6,194 meters)

•

World's largest island: Greenland

•

Location of North Magnetic Pole

North America
Terrain

North America has several mountainous areas. The western mountains are made up of two main chains that stretch from Alaska at the northern end of the continent to Panama at the southern end. The Rocky Mountains rise out of the Great Plains. The Rockies reach into Canada, where they are even more spectacular than they are in the United States.

The Great Basin lies between the two western mountain chains in the United States. Mountains prevent most of the Pacific moisture from reaching the Great Basin,

Coral reefs and submarine volcanoes formed the islands of the Caribbean. Many of the coral islands are flat and low-lying, while those of volcanic origin tend to be rugged. Shown here is volcanic Saba in the Leeward Islands.

© 1979 Rand McNally & Co.

British Columbia is the westernmost province of Canada. Its mountainous terrain once isolated it from the rest of the country. Today it is the site of several national parks, including Yoho National Park, shown here.

Monument Valley lies on the border between Utah and Arizona. Here sandstone buttes, mesas, and arches rise above the sandy plain below—some as high as one thousand feet (three hundred meters).

and the southern end of the basin is a desert. Farther south, a desertlike region covers much of the American Southwest and reaches deep into Mexico.

The two mountain chains extend into Mexico as well. The Sierra Madre Occidental is in the west, and the Sierra Madre Oriental is in the east. Plateau country spreads out between them, and it is here that most Mexicans live. Central America, at the south end of North America, is mainly mountainous.

The mountains of eastern North America are much lower than the ones to the west. Some of them are older mountains, and they have been worn down by time and weather. One such range is the Appalachians, the biggest mountain range in the eastern United States.

The Great Plains lie at the center of North America. This region is one of the largest plains on Earth, and the land is mostly flat or gently rolling as far as the eye can see.

North America has several important rivers and bodies of water. The Mississippi and Missouri rivers form the longest river system on the continent. Lake Superior, one of the five Great Lakes, is the largest freshwater lake in the world. The Panama Canal, near the southern tip of North America, is a human-made strip of water that allows ships to pass between the Atlantic and the Pacific oceans without having to go all the way around the southern tip of South America.

Animals

As the number of people in North America has increased, the number of wild animals has decreased. People have hunted some animals to extinction.

The buffalo, or American bison, was once nearly wiped out by hunters. The pronghorn antelope had a similar fate. Conservation efforts kept both species from extinction, and today they are found in protected areas on the Great Plains.

Wolves and mighty grizzly bears prowl in the north. The bald eagle, the national bird of the United States, is still found in the Northwest. These animals are endangered today.

The coyote, a symbol of the American West, preys on prairie dogs, mice, rabbits, and sometimes on livestock. Raccoons can be found from southern Canada to South America, except in parts of the Rockies and in deserts. Looking like a masked bandit, the raccoon forages at night and will feed on garbage. Both animals seem to thrive near people.

Many kinds of rattlesnakes, named for the rattles on their tails, inhabit North America. The largest of them is the eastern diamondback, often seven feet (over two meters) long. The coral snake, a colorful relative of the cobra, also lives in the deserts, as does a poisonous lizard called the Gila monster.

In the swamps and rivers of the southeastern part of the continent lives the alligator. These meat-eating reptiles can reach nine feet (2.7 meters) in length. Hunted for their skins, alligators are now protected.

It has been said that most of the animals that have ever lived on earth are now extinct. We know about prehistoric animals only from their fossil remains. Extinctions still occur, some of them the result of human interference. The passenger pigeon was seen and painted by John James Audubon in 1840.

Apatosaurus
135 Million Years Ago

Tyrannosaurus
70 Million Years Ago

Woolly Mammoth
10 Thousand Years Ago

Great Auk
Mid Nineteenth Century

Saber-Toothed Cat
1 Million Years Ago

Passenger Pigeon
Late Nineteenth Century

Grizzly Bear

Walrus

Herring Gull

Canada Goose

Polar Bear

Red Fox

Gray Wolf

Mountain Goat

Rock Ptarmigan

Beaver

Bald Eagle

Porcupine

Mountain Lion

Moose

Robin

King Salmon

Pronghorn

Gray Squirrel

Elk

Raccoon

White-tailed Deer

Sea Otter

Bison

Cottontail

Willet

Gambel's Quail

Diamondback Rattlesnake

Opossum

Turkey

California Sea Lions

Peccary

Alligator

Armadillo

Roseate Spoonbill

Brown Pelican

Squirrel Monkey

Gray Whale

Life on the Land

Ice hockey is a popular sport played by both amateurs and professionals in Canada and the United States, as well as in other countries. Hockey is the national sport of Canada.

The United States and Canada, two of the three largest countries in North America, are also among the richest nations in the world. Many. factors contribute to this abundant wealth, including agriculture. North America has much fertile farmland and a good climate for growing a variety of crops.

Rich mineral deposits also contribute to the prosperity of the United States and Canada. Mineral exports from these countries include copper, lead, asbestos, zinc, silver, nickel, coal, crude oil, and natural gas.

North America's rich forests and mineral reserves have helped the United States and Canada to become world leaders in manufacturing. Many cities in these countries have been huge industrial centers for many years, but this is gradually changing.

Agriculture is very important in Mexico and in other countries of North America as well. Corn is grown in Mexico. In Central America and the islands called the West Indies, coffee, sugarcane, and bananas are grown. But much of the land in these countries is not good for growing crops, and many of the farmers do not have modern machinery.

There is not as much manufacturing in the other countries of North America, although the iron, steel, and chemical industries are growing. Mexico is also a leading producer of silver and petroleum. Tourists, interested in the country's sunny climate and ancient ruins, also help the economy.

According to folklore, the giant Paul Bunyan and his enormous blue ox Babe created much of America's landscape. The legend claims that they dug the St. Lawrence River in three weeks using a shovel as large as a house.

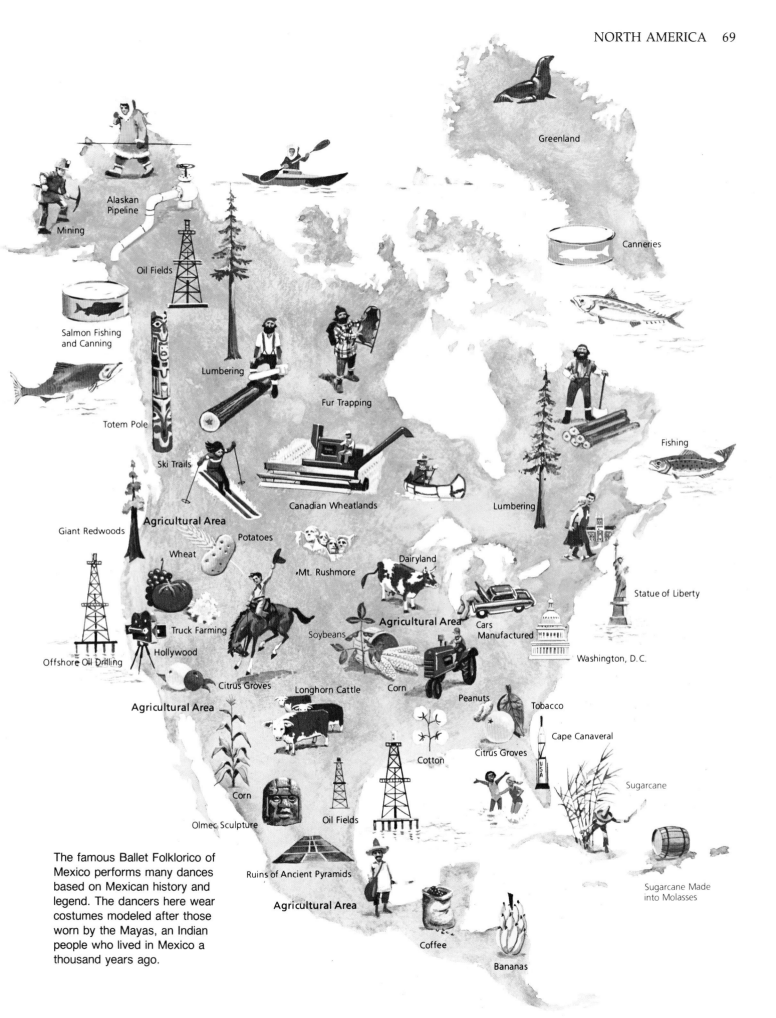

Greenland

Canneries

Mining

Alaskan Pipeline

Oil Fields

Salmon Fishing and Canning

Lumbering

Fur Trapping

Totem Pole

Lumbering

Fishing

Ski Trails

Canadian Wheatlands

Agricultural Area

Giant Redwoods

Wheat

Potatoes

Mt. Rushmore

Dairyland

Statue of Liberty

Truck Farming

Agricultural Area

Soybeans

Cars Manufactured

Offshore Oil Drilling

Hollywood

Washington, D.C.

Citrus Groves

Longhorn Cattle

Corn

Peanuts

Tobacco

Agricultural Area

Cotton

Citrus Groves

Cape Canaveral

Corn

Sugarcane

Olmec Sculpture

Oil Fields

Ruins of Ancient Pyramids

Agricultural Area

Sugarcane Made into Molasses

The famous Ballet Folklorico of Mexico performs many dances based on Mexican history and legend. The dancers here wear costumes modeled after those worn by the Mayas, an Indian people who lived in Mexico a thousand years ago.

Coffee

Bananas

NORTH AMERICA
Countries and Cities

Mexico City is the capital and fastest-growing city of that nation. It is among the five most populous cities of the world. In 1985, the city suffered a major earthquake, which caused much damage and killed thousands.

Of all the continents, the boundaries between countries are the simplest in North America. Most of the continent is divided among three nations: Canada, the United States, and Mexico. Central America, considered a part of North America, covers an area less than a third the size of Mexico and contains seven countries.

The countries of North America are mainly inhabited by descendants of Europeans who crossed the seas after the 1500s. Native Americans, the people who lived here long before the Europeans arrived, still populate some areas and many live close to the way their ancestors lived.

Like the people of the conti-nent's three largest nations, most North Americans elect their leaders. In some countries, such as Panama, military leaders have taken control of the government. For Panama, at least, this may now be changing. Cuba, an island nation in the Caribbean, has long had a communist government.

The main language of each North American nation is the language spoken in the European country that once dominated the area. For example, Spain once ruled Mexico, and although Mexico is now independent, its people still speak Spanish.

Cities usually grow up around areas that are accessible to trade routes, and the cities of North America are no exception. Many of them sprung up near bodies of water that were traveled by the many traders who explored the land. For example, Chicago, Illinois, grew up on a

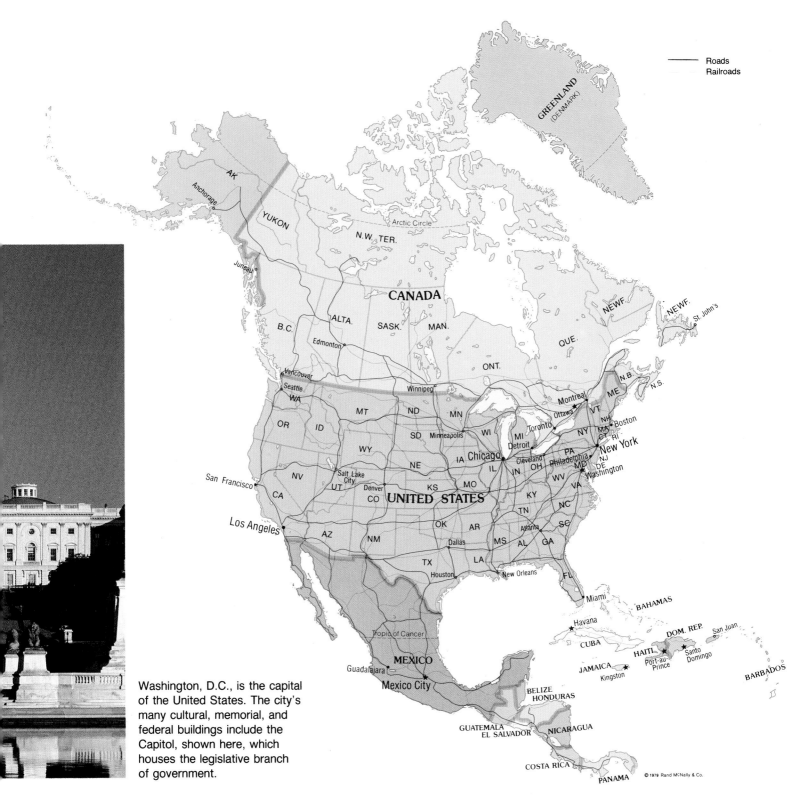

Roads
Railroads

Washington, D.C., is the capital of the United States. The city's many cultural, memorial, and federal buildings include the Capitol, shown here, which houses the legislative branch of government.

crossroads that linked the Great Lakes and the Mississippi River. Detroit, Toronto, Ottawa, and Cleveland have a similar history.

Today, some of the biggest and most modern cities in the world are in North America. The population of New York City is one of the largest in the world. With over 8.8 million people, Mexico City is even larger. In fact, Mexico is the most populous Spanish-speaking country in the world and carries much influence with those nations.

B
A

DISTRICT
VICTORIA ISLAND
NORTH WEST TERRITORY
DISTRICT OF MACKENZIE
DISTRICT

C. BARING
Prince Albert Sound
WOLLASTON PEN.
Dolphin and Union Str.
Dease Strait
KENT PEN.
Coronation Gulf
Cambridge Bay
KING WILLIAM I.
Queen Maud Gulf
Chantrey Inlet
Simpson Str.
Pelly Bay
BOOTHIA PENINSULA
Bathurst Inlet
Back
Garry
Pelly
Chesterfield Inlet
Baker Lake
Chesterfield In'l
Rankin Inlet
Dubawnt
Yathkyed
Nueltin
Selwyn
Thanne
Tha-anne
Seal
Churchill

MELVILLE HILLS
Amundsen Gulf
Eskimo Lakes
Anderson
Mackenzie
C. Baring
Inuvik
Tuktoyaktuk
Aklavik
Ft. McPherson
Ft. Good Hope
Arctic Circle
Coppermine
Port Radium
PEACOCK HILLS
Contwoyto
MacKay
Aylmer
Clinton-Colden
Baker Lake
Great Bear Lake
Norman Wells
FRANKLIN MTS.
Lac la Martre
Yellowknife
Ft. Providence
Great Slave Lake
Nonacho
HORN PLATEAU
Ft. Simpson
Ft. Liard
CAMERON HILLS
Ft. Resolution
Hay River
Ft. Smith
Ft. Fitzgerald
WOOD BUFFALO NAT'L PARK
Uranium City
Selwyn
Wollaston
Reindeer
Southern Indian
Granville
Amery
Churchill

ALASKA
U.S.A.
CANADA
KLONDIKE REGION
OGILVIE MTS.
RICHARDSON MTS.
Old Crow
Porcupine
Dawson
YUKON
Stewart
Mayo
Whitehorse
PELLY MTS.
Carcross
Skagway
White Pass
Watson Lake
MACKENZIE MTS.
NAHANNI NAT'L PARK
Frances
Telegraph Creek
Churchill Peak
Ft. Nelson
Ft. Liard
Norman Wells
CHICHAGOF
Juneau
Douglas
Sitka
BARANOF
STIKINE RANGES
COAST
ROCKY
MOUNTAINS
BRITISH
COLUMBIA
CARIBOO MTS.
MONASHEE
SELKIRK MTS.

PRINCE OF WALES I.
Ketchikan
Prince Rupert
Dixon Entrance
DALL I.
QUEEN CHARLOTTE ISLANDS
Masset
GRAHAM I.
Hecate Strait
Queen Charlotte
MORESBY ISLAND
Hazelton
Smithers
Kitimat
Terrace
Ocean Falls
CALVERT
CAPE SCOTT
Port Alice
Campbell River
Courtenay
NOOTKA
Port Alberni
Nanaimo
Duncan
VANCOUVER ISLAND
Port Hardy
CAPE FLATTERY
Str. of Juan de Fuca
Victoria
Burnaby
Vancouver
North Vancouver
Chilliwack
Hope
SEATTLE
Tacoma
Olympia
Vancouver
Portland
Salem
Eugene
Astoria
WASHINGTON
OREGON
IDAHO
CASCADE RANGE
Mt. Rainier 14,410
Mt. Adams 12,307
Yakima
Spokane
Moscow
Walla Walla
Pendleton
Baker
Snake
Columbia
BITTERROOT RANGE
Great Falls
Helena
Butte
Billings
MONTANA
LITTLE BELT MTS.
BIG BELT MTS.
Granite Peak 12,799
Yellowstone
WYO.
SOUTH DAKOTA
NORTH DAKOTA
Bismarck
Valley City
Fargo
Grand Forks
Minot
Williston
Missouri
Milk
GOOSE
Govenlock

Fort Nelson
ALASKA HIGHWAY
Ft. St. John
Dawson Creek
Peace
FORT
Hazelton
Ft. St. James
Vanderhoof
Prince George
Burns Lake
Fraser
Quesnel
Wells
McBride
Mt. Robson
JASPER NAT'L PARK
Valemount
Blue River
GLACIER NAT'L PARK
MT. REVELSTOKE NAT'L PARK
Revelstoke
BANFF NAT'L PARK
Golden
Lillooet
Clinton
Kamloops
Merritt
Princeton
Hope
Penticton
Vernon
Kelowna
OKANAGAN
Oliver
Grand Forks
Rossland
Trail
Nelson
Creston
Kimberley
Cranbrook
Fernie
Sparwood
KOOTENAY NAT'L PARK
YOHO NAT'L PARK
Calgary
Banff
Radium Hot Springs
High River
Claresholm
Fort Macleod
Lethbridge
Cardston
Magrath
WATERTON GLACIER INT'L PEACE PARK
Taber
Medicine Hat
Redcliff
CANADA
U.S.A.

CLEAR HILLS
BUFFALO HEAD HILLS
CARIBOU MTS.
Ft. Vermilion
BIRCH MTS.
Ft. Chipewyan
L. Claire
Athabasca
Fort McMurray
CHEECHAM HILLS
Peter Pond Lake
Peace River
McLennan
High Prairie
Grouard Mission
Lesser Slave Lake
Smith
Athabasca
SWAN HILLS
Grande Prairie
ALBERTA
Whitecourt
Barrhead
Lac la Biche
Beaver
Westlock
Edson
ELK ISLAND NAT'L PARK
Edmonton
St. Paul
Meadow Lake
Big River
St. Walburg
PRINCE ALBERT NAT'L PARK
Jasper
Mountain Park
Wetaskiwin
Camrose
Vegreville
Vermilion
Lloydminster
North Battleford
Prince Albert
Nipawin
Melfort
Tisdale
Ponoka
Wainwright
Lacombe
Red Deer
Innisfail
Stettler
Wilkie
Biggar
Saskatoon
Humboldt
SASKATCHEWAN
Flin Flon
Lynn Lake
Cross
Sipiwesk
Thompson
MANITOBA
Norway House
Berens River
Gods
Olds
Drumheller
Hanna
Kindersley
Rosetown
Lanigan
Big Quill
Watrous
Wynyard
Canora
Kamsack
Yorkton
Melville
Russell
DUCK MTN.
RIDING MOUNTAIN NAT'L PARK
Dauphin
Swan River
Gypsumville
Winnipegosis
Lake Winnipegosis
Neepawa
Minnedosa
Portage la Prairie
Selkirk
Beausejour
Lake Winnipeg
Bassano
Red Deer
Swift Current
Diefenbaker
Last Mountain
Moose Jaw
Regina
Qu'Appelle
Indian Head
Maple Creek
Gravelbourg
Assiniboia
Shaunavon
Weyburn
Estevan
Souris
Boissevain
Carman
Morden
Morris
Winnipeg
Steinbach
Emerson

PACIFIC OCEAN

Cities, Towns, and Villages

0 to 25,000 ○	100,000 to 250,000 ⊙	1,000,000 and over ◉
25,000 to 100,000 ●	250,000 to 1,000,000 ⊚	Major urbanized area

Scale 1:12,600,000; one inch to 200 miles. Conic Projection
Elevations and depressions are given in feet

14 80° 15 75° 16 70° 17 18 60° 19 55° 20 21 Longitude West of Greenwich 55° 23

Inset map (upper right):

60°
QUEBEC
Gulf of
St. Lawrence
CAPE BAULD
C. ST. JOHN
LONG RANGE MTS.
Notre Dame Bay
GROS MORNE NAT'L PARK
Deer Lake
Twillingate
Corner Brook
Borwood
Windsor
Stephenville
Grand Falls
Gander
Bonavista
TERRA NOVA NAT'L PARK
C. ST. GEORGE
St. George's Bay
St. George s
NEWFOUNDLAND
Trinity
Channel-Port-aux-Basques
CAPE RAY
Grand Bank
Burin
CAPE NORTH
Fortune Bay
Placentia Bay
St. John's
CAPE BRETON ISLAND
ST. PIERRE AND MIQUELON (Fr.)
ATLANTIC OCEAN
©RMCN.
Same scale as main map
h
k

Main map labels:

Igloolik
FRANKLIN
BAFFIN ISLAND NAT'L PARK
Pangnirtung
CUMBERLAND PEN.
B
MELVILLE PENINSULA
Foxe Basin
PRINCE CHARLES ISLAND
BAFFIN ISLAND
Nettilling
Amadjuak
Arctic Circle
Cumberland Sound
C
Foxe Channel
Mercy
FOXE PEN.
Iqaluit
HALL PEN.
Frobisher Bay
Lake Harbour
EVERETT MTS.
SOUTHAMPTON ISLAND
SALISBURY
C. DE NOUVELLE-FRANCE
Hudson
Strait
RESOLUTION
C. LOW
Fisher Strait
COATS
NOTTINGHAM ISLAND
C. HOPES ADVANCE
AKPATOK
KILLINIQ I.
TORNGAT MTS.
Hebron
E
MANSEL
Ivujivik
KEEWATIN
PENINSULE D'UNGAVA
Ungava Bay
Kuujjuaq
Nain
NEWFOU
Hopedale
Makkovik
Hamilton Inlet
Povungnituk
Payne
Rigolet
Cartwright
HUDSON BAY
OTTAWA ISLANDS
aux Feuilles
Koksoak
Can.
Michikamau
Naskaupi
MEALY MTS.
Battle Harbour
Kaniapiskau
Happy Valley
Goose Bay
LABRADOR
St. Anthony
All islands within bays and straits lie within Northwest Territories.
Minto
Schefferville
Churchill Falls
Little Mecatina
LONG RANGE MTS.
BELCHER ISLANDS
Grande de la Baleine
Lac Bienville
Caniapiscau
NEWFOUNDLAND
Corner Brook
Stephenville
St. George
Ft. Severn
C. HENRIETTA MARIA
PTE. LOUIS-XIV
La Grande
Nichicun
Lac Ashuanipi
QUEBEC
Romaine
GROS MORNE NAT'L PARK
Natashquan
Opinaca
Caniapiscau
Eastmain
MTS. OTISH
aux Outardes
Mingan
ILE D'ANTICOSTI
F
James Bay
Chisasibi
Nottaway
Rupert
Clarke City
Sept-Iles
Gulf of
AKIMISKI
Mistassini
Manicouagan
Lac Manicouagan
St. Lawrence
Channel Port-aux-Basques
CAPE BRETON HIGHLANDS NAT'L PARK
Ft. Albany
Chibougamau
St. Maurice
Betsiamites
Cap-Chat
MTS. CHIC-CHOCS
PEN. DE GASPE
Chandler
ILES DE LA MADELEINE
Sydney Mines
North Sydney
Moosonee
Harricana
Dolbeau
Alma
Rimouski
Matane
New Carlisle
Sydney
ONTARIO
Coral Rapids
Fraserdale
Nemiscau
St. Félicien
Roberval
Kénogami
Chicoutimi
Saguenay
Mont-Joli
Campbellton
Rivière-du-Loup
Newcastle
Edmundston
NEW BRUNSWICK
Chatham
Caraquet
P.E.I.
Summerside
PRINCE EDWARD ISLAND NAT'L PARK
New Glasgow
Antigonish
Lac Seul
Red Lake
Armstrong Sta.
Nakina
Hearst
La Sarre
Amos
Senneterre
Chambord
Jonquière
La Malbaie
Boie-St. Paul
CANADA U.S.A.
Woodstock
Fredericton
Richibucto
Moncton
NOVA SCOTIA
Sioux Lookout
Geraldton
Longlac
Kapuskasing
Oba
Cochrane
Iroquois Falls
Rouyn
Val-d'Or
Parent
La Tuque
Québec
Lévis
Shawinigan
FUNDY NAT'L PARK
Springhill
Stellarton
Truro
Dryden
Nipigon
Marathon
Timmins
Kirkland Lake
Malartic
Trois-Rivières
Grand Mère
Victoriaville
St. Jean
Saint John
St. George
St. Andrews
Kentville
Windsor
Dartmouth
Halifax
Lac St. Jean
Lac-Frontière
St. Stephen
MAINE
Chapleau
Cobalt
Ville-Marie
Témiscaming
Joliette
Sorel
Drummondville
Sherbrooke
Augusta
Digby
Lunenburg
Bridgewater
Liverpool
Shelburne
G
PUKASKWA NAT'L PARK
MICHIPICOTEN I.
Sudbury
Surgeon Falls
North Bay
Mattawa
Ottawa
Hull
MONTRÉAL
St. Jean
Granby
VERMONT
NEW HAMPSHIRE
Montpelier
Portland
Yarmouth
CAPE SABLE
Thunder Bay
Blind River
Espanola
Pembroke
Renfrew
Smiths Falls
Brockville
Ogdensburg
Concord
BOSTON
CAPE COD
Lake Superior
Sault Ste. Marie
Thessalon
Sault Ste. Marie
Georgian Bay
Parry Sound
Huntsville
Bancroft
Kingston
Alexandria Bay
Champlain
Lake
ATLANTIC OCEAN
Marquette
Escanaba
MANITOULIN I.
Wiarton
Midland
Orillia
Peterborough
Lindsay
Cobourg
Trenton
NEW YORK
Albany
MASS.
Hartford
R.I. Providence
CONN.
Duluth
Superior
Owen Sound
Barrie
Simcoe
Oshawa
Rochester
ESOTA
WISCONSIN
MICHIGAN
Kincardine
Lake Huron
Lake Ontario
TORONTO
Whitby
Hamilton
Niagara Falls
BUFFALO
NEW YORK
New York
N.J.
St. Paul
Green Bay
Saginaw
Flint
Kitchener
London
St. Catharines
Rochester
Scranton
PENNSYLVANIA
NNEAPOLIS
Madison
MILWAUKEE
Grand Rapids
Lansing
DETROIT
Windsor
Port Huron
Sarnia
Chatham
Leamington
St. Thomas
ILL.
CHICAGO
Toledo
OHIO
Lake Michigan
Lake Erie

H-520200-26-
COPYRIGHT BY
RAND McNALLY & COMPANY
MADE IN U.S.A.

Scale bars:

0 25 50 75 100 200 300 400 500 Miles
0 100 200 400 600 800 Kilometers

Inset (lower right):

17
40,000 SQ MI AREA
0 100 200
Miles

12 15 16

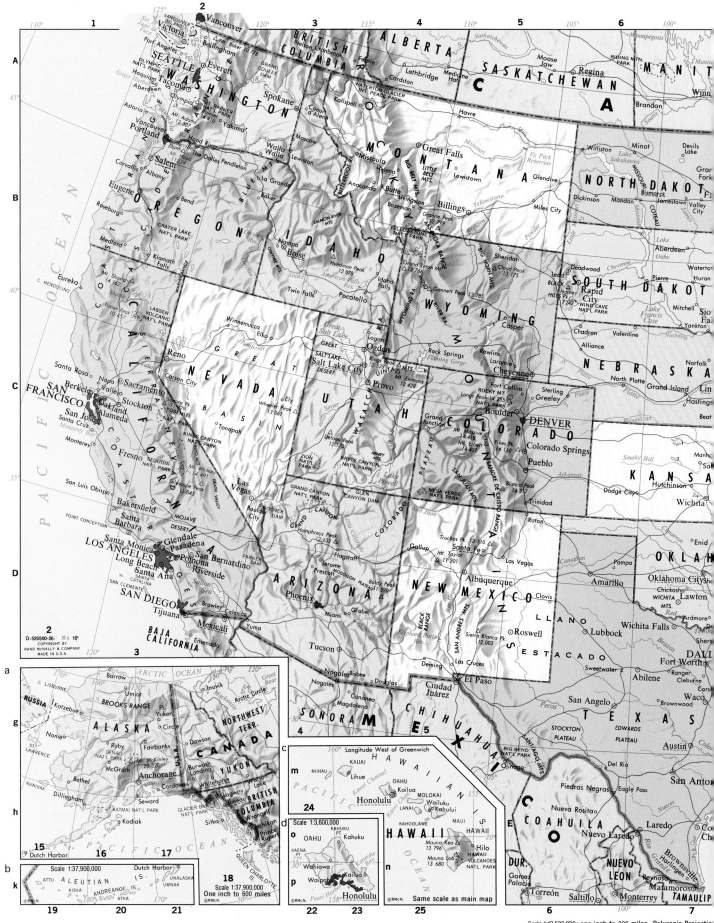

Scale 1:12,600,000; one inch to 200 miles. Polyconic Projection
Elevations and depressions are given in feet

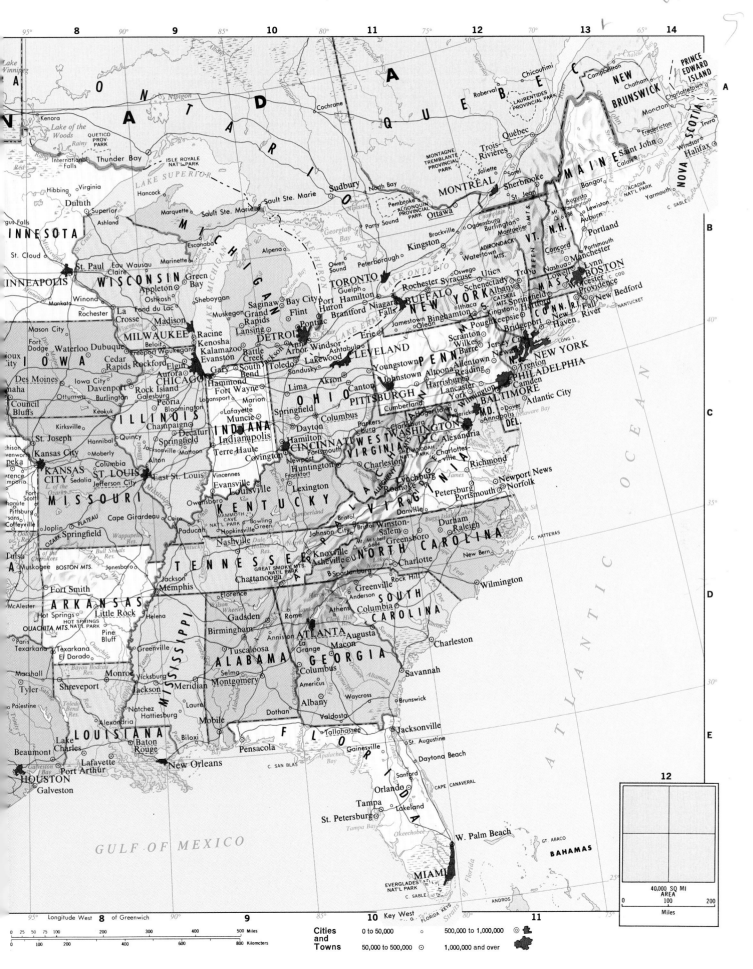

ONTARIO
QUEBEC
NEW BRUNSWICK
PRINCE EDWARD ISLAND
NOVA SCOTIA
MAINE
N.H.
VT.
MASS.
CONN. R.I.
NEW YORK
PENN.
OHIO
INDIANA
ILLINOIS
WISCONSIN
MICHIGAN
IOWA
MISSOURI
KENTUCKY
WEST VIRGINIA
VIRGINIA
NORTH CAROLINA
SOUTH CAROLINA
TENNESSEE
ARKANSAS
MISSISSIPPI
ALABAMA
GEORGIA
LOUISIANA
FLORIDA
MINNESOTA
MD.
DEL.
N.J.

GULF OF MEXICO
ATLANTIC OCEAN
BAHAMAS

Lake Winnipeg
Lake of the Woods
Lake Superior
Lake Michigan
Lake Huron
Lake Erie
Lake Ontario

MONTREAL
Ottawa
TORONTO
BUFFALO
DETROIT
CLEVELAND
PITTSBURGH
CHICAGO
MILWAUKEE
MINNEAPOLIS
St. Paul
ST. LOUIS
KANSAS CITY
CINCINNATI
WASHINGTON D.C.
BALTIMORE
PHILADELPHIA
NEW YORK
BOSTON
ATLANTA
HOUSTON
New Orleans
MIAMI

	12

40,000 SQ MI AREA
0   100   200
Miles

Key West

Cities and Towns

0 to 50,000
50,000 to 500,000
500,000 to 1,000,000
1,000,000 and over

0 25 50 75 100   200   300   400   500 Miles
0   100   200   400   600   800 Kilometers

Scale 1:17,200,000; one inch to 270 miles. Polyconic Projection
Elevations and depressions are given in feet

H-530000-26- ·10-23⁴
COPYRIGHT BY
RAND McNALLY & COMPANY
MADE IN U.S.A.

Scale 1:1,080,000

PANAMA

South America
Terrain

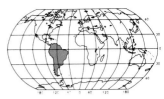

South America

Fourth largest continent

•

Fifth in population: 310,700,000

•

31 cities with over 1 million population

•

Highest mountain: Aconcagua,
22,831 feet (6,959 meters)

•

World's highest waterfall: Angel Falls,
3,212 feet (979 meters)

•

Equator passes through

Kaieteur National Park in central Guyana lies in a region of forested highlands and plateaus. Wind and water have molded the park's sandstone and shale into a variety of interesting formations.

The Sierra of Peru is a high-altitude region of gentle slopes surrounded by the towering peaks of the Andes. Farmland is found between the mountains; this is a farming community near the Urubamba River.

The Andes Mountains run down the entire western side of South America. Stretching more than four thousand miles (about 6,500 kilometers), the Andes chain is the longest in the world. This range also has some of the world's tallest peaks. Only the Himalayas in Asia are higher than Argentina's Mount Aconcagua.

Where Argentina, Bolivia, and Chile meet, the Andes split into two ranges. They are separated by a plateau about four hundred miles (about 650 kilometers) wide. This is called the Altiplano, or high plateau.

In northern Chile, between the Andes and the Pacific, is the Atacama Desert. This de-sert is near the ocean, yet it is one of the driest spots on earth. In some parts of the Atacama, no rainfall has ever been recorded.

Many rivers and streams tumble from the Andes and other highland areas. The Amazon River begins in the Andes of Peru and flows almost four thousand miles (more than six thousand kilometers) to the Atlantic Ocean. The Amazon contains more water than any other river on earth. Over four million cubic feet (more than 113,000 cubic meters) pour out of the Amazon and into the Atlantic each second. The stream of fresh water from the river can be detected in the ocean for about a hun-

West of the Paraguay River lies the Gran Chaco, a region of dry plains with a climate harsher than that of eastern Paraguay. The nation's large cattle ranches are found here.

dred miles (160 kilometers) off the coast of South America.

The Amazon flows out of a huge plain called the Amazon River basin, an area almost as big as the United States. The equator runs through this area, so it is very warm, and it re-

ceives a lot of rainfall. These factors combine to make this region the biggest tropical rain forest on earth.

A plain stretches across Paraguay and most of Argentina. It is made up of two different areas—the Gran Chaco and

the Pampa. The Gran Chaco is a dry region with few trees. The Pampa receives more rain; it is a nearly treeless grassland ideal for grazing cattle and sheep. Patagonia lies near the southern tip of South America.

Animals

Nearly a fourth of all the species of animals known live in South America. But as in other parts of the world, people are hunting these animals and attempting to develop the lands the animals live on, so many creatures are in danger of becoming extinct.

The Amazon rain forests provide homes for many animals. The jaguar, a big spotted cat, prowls among the trees at night, and herds of piglike peccaries root in the underbrush. The tapir, an animal that looks like a large hog with a long nose, also lives in the forest.

The trees of the rain forest brighten with the colorful plumage of parrots, macaws, toucans, and other birds. Monkeys howl and shriek from the treetops. Sloths hang upside down from the branches and feed on leaves at night. The boa constrictor also lives in the rain forest.

In the rivers swim caimans, the alligators of South America. Schools of razor-toothed fish called piranha cruise through the water.

On the plains of South America live giant anteaters, which may be more than six feet (about two meters) long. The long-legged maned wolf live here, too.

In the Andes live llamas, vicuñas, and alpacas. Some of these animals have been tamed by people who use them like sheep or cattle. The spectacled bear lives on mountain slopes. It gets its name from the circles of yellowish fur, like eyeglass frames, around its eyes.

The mysterious Galapagos Islands lie about 600 miles (965.58 kilometers) off the coast of Ecuador. Here live rare cormorants that cannot fly, great lizardlike iguanas, and giant turtles weighing 500 pounds (226.8 kilograms). Some species have been victimized by overhunting, but the islands are now a national park and wildlife refuge.

Sloth

Tapir

Manatee

Scarlet Ibis

Coatimundi

Ocelot

Piranha

Green Turtle

Toucan

Caiman

Spectacled Bear

Anaconda

Llama

Spider Monkey

Red Brocket Deer

Vampire Bat

Capybara

Jaguar

Howling Monkey

Macaw

Chinchilla

Great Anteater

Vicuña

Brazilian Lapwing

Condor

Guanaco

Maned Wolf

Blue Marlin

Alpaca

Pampas Deer

Torrent Duck

Rhea

Elephant Seal

Magellan Goose

Magellan Penguin

Cavy

Black-necked Swan

Sperm Whale

Life on the Land

Close to half of all South Americans make their living by farming. Most farms are quite small and can produce only enough food for the families that own them. Most of these people use old-fashioned ways of farming, with no machinery. There are huge modern farms and ranches, however, and they are owned by a small number of wealthy people. Some of these farms are larger than many of the states of the United States. The farms grow huge quantities of coffee, cacao, wheat, sugar, bananas, rice, and other food.

The rain forests—hot, moist, and thick with vegetation— might seem to be an ideal place for farming. But, cleared of trees, the jungle soil loses the important nutrients crops need to grow. Much of the rain forest has been cut down in a futile attempt to create farmland. Herds of sheep and beef cattle are raised on giant ranches. Argentina is one of the largest producers of beef in the world.

Drilling rigs in Venezuela and Ecuador jab into the earth and bring up crude oil. These two nations are the largest oil exporters in South America.

Life in the big cities of South America is much like life in the cities of North America. There are tall, modern buildings, airports, and busy streets. But many of the Indians outside of the cities of Peru, Bolivia, and Ecuador still live the way their ancestors lived. And in the rain forest, some people live as they have for thousands of years.

Over four hundred years ago, the empire of the Incas thrived in the Andes. Legend has it that the first Incas, Manco Capac and his sister, were created from the sun god on the Isle of the Sun in Lake Titicaca.

Weaving is an age-old art in the Andes, one passed down from generation to generation. Indians spin thick alpaca wool into yarn to make warm blankets, hats, and other clothing.

Soccer, or *fútbol* in Spanish, is one of the world's most widely played sports. It is the national sport of several South American countries.

Oil Exported

Oil Fields

Coffee Bean Farming

Emerald Mining

Fishing

Mining

Shipping

Agricultural Area

The Amazon

Rubber

Mahogany Logging

Brazil Nuts Harvested

Cotton

Spanish-style Architecture

Indians of Peru

Machu Picchu (Inca Ruins)

Fishing in Lake Titicaca

Soccer

Agricultural Area

Anchovy Fishing

Brasilia

Mining

Mining

Trees Tapped for Tannin

Light Industry

Rio de Janeiro

Copper

Coffee Grown

Agricultural Area

Cattle Raising

Beef for Export

Fishing

Wheatlands

Bonito Fishing

Lumbering and Sawmills

Sheep Herding

SOUTH AMERICA
Countries and Cities

Ancestors of Native Americans crossed a narrow bridge of land between what is now Alaska and Siberia thousands of years ago. Over the centuries, the American Indians populated all of North and South America. In the Andes Mountains, a sophisticated Native American group called the Incas thrived and created a huge empire. The lands that now make up the nations of Peru, Ecuador, and Bolivia were part of the empire. Cuzco, Peru, was its capital.

Just like North America, South America was explored and conquered by Europeans after about 1500. People from Spain, Portugal, and other European countries took over the land, some of which had been inhabited by Indians for centu-

Roads
Railroads

Suriname's bauxite deposits fuel the nation's mining and industry. Much of the bauxite is shipped to the United States, but Suriname's factories also process the ore into alumina and aluminum for export.

ries. Many wars were fought over the years, but the borders of many of today's South American countries have existed for over one hundred years.

South America's largest and most populated country is Brazil. More people live in Brazil than in all other South American countries combined. Brazil is also the continent's leading industrial nation. Argentina is the second-largest South American country.

Like North Americans, most South Americans speak the language of the European country that once ruled the area in which they live. For example, Brazil was once a colony of Portugal, and today most Brazilians speak Portuguese. Many other South American countries were once dominated by Spain, and Spanish is widely spoken on the continent. There are many American Indians in South America who still speak the languages of their ancestors.

South America has many important cities. The biggest of them is São Paulo, Brazil—one of the largest cities in the world. Buenos Aires, Argentina, and Rio de Janeiro, Brazil, are also in the world's top ten in population. All three cities are very modern and have a lot of industry. If you look at these three cities on the map, you see they all have something in common: they are all near the Atlantic coast. They all grew up around or very close to natural ports, or places where ships could safely land.

Inhabited before the eleventh century, Quito, Ecuador, is situated in the Andes, only fifteen miles (twenty-four kilometers) south of the equator. The city is the capital and second largest city in Ecuador.

The second largest city in Brazil and one of the most populous in the world, Rio de Janeiro is a popular tourist destination.

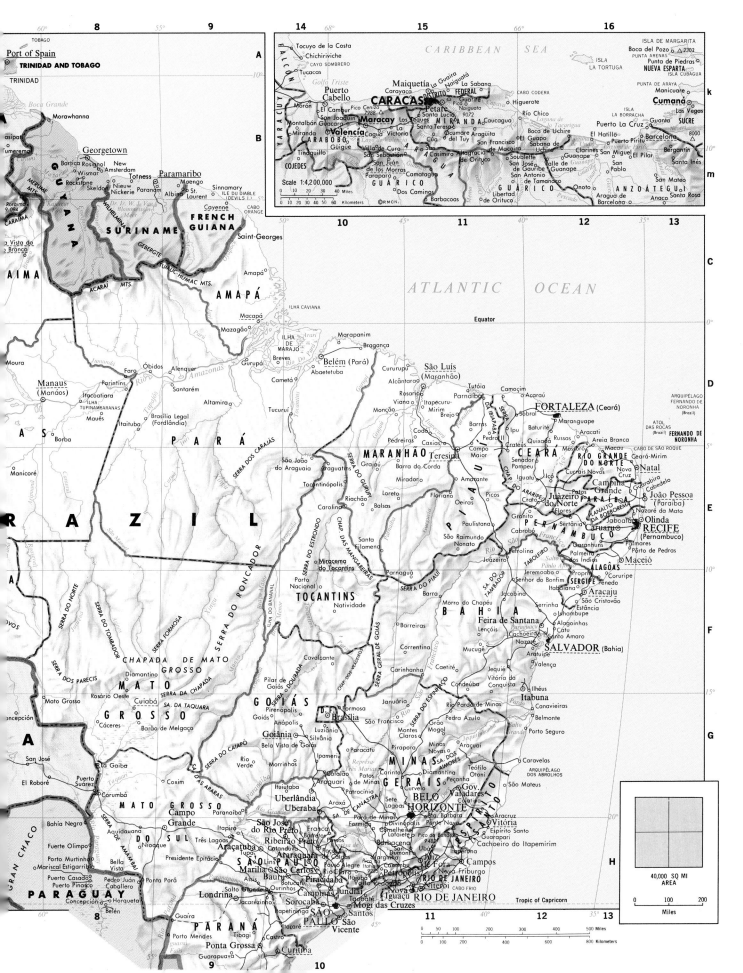

Antarctica
The South Pole

Antarctica

Fifth largest continent

•

No permanent population

•

Highest mountain: Vinson Massif,
16,864 feet (5,140.14 meters)

•

Location of South Pole

•

Location of South Magnetic Pole

•

World's lowest recorded temperature:
Vostok, -129°F (-89°C)

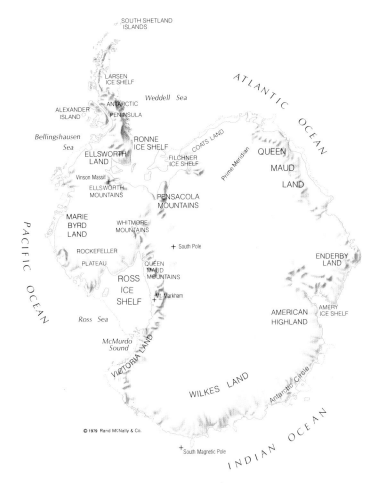

Antarctica, the coldest continent on earth, rests squarely on the South Pole. It is so cold here that a person without the right kind of clothing would freeze to death in a matter of minutes. In midwinter, which is June in the Southern Hemisphere, temperatures may drop below −100° F (−73° C).

Like some places north of the Arctic Circle, Antarctica is without sunlight for part of the year. This happens because the earth's spin axis, which runs through the North and South poles like the axle of a wheel, tilts into the plane of the planet's orbit. A visitor at the South Pole would enjoy six months of never-ending daylight during the summer—and six months of frigid, never-ending night during winter.

Even in the summer the sun gives the continent little heat. Most of Antarctica is covered with snow heaped so thick it forms a mile-high plateau at the pole.

Microscopic creatures teem in the waters around Antarctica, but large animals can be found there as well. Among these are seals, birds, and the 150-ton (135-metric-ton) blue whale.

Antarctica is the home of many penguins. Though penguins are birds, they cannot fly. Their wings are used as paddles to help them move underwater.

In 1911, explorers discovered the South Pole. Today, no one makes a permanent home on this frozen continent, but hundreds of scientists study Antarctica's unique environment.

Penguins frolic in the cold waters off the coast of Antarctica. These are adélie penguins, one of only two species that breed in Antarctica.

World Facts and Comparisons

General Information

Mean distance from the earth to the sun, 93,020,000 miles.
Mean distance from the earth to the moon, 238,857 miles.
Equatorial diameter of the earth, 7,926.38 miles.
Polar diameter of the earth, 7,899.80 miles.
Mean diameter of the earth, 7,917.52 miles.
Equatorial circumference of the earth, 24,901.46 miles.
Polar circumference of the earth, 24,855.34 miles.

Total area of the earth, 197,000,000 square miles.
Total land area of the earth (incl. inland water and Antarctica), 57,900,000 square miles.
Highest elevation on the earth's surface, Mt. Everest, Asia, 29,028 feet.
Lowest elevation on the earth's land surface, shores of the Dead Sea, Asia, 1,312 feet below sea level.
Greatest known depth of the ocean, southwest of Guam, Pacific Ocean, 35,810 feet.
Area of Africa, 11,700,000 square miles.

Area of Antarctica, 5,400,000 square miles.
Area of Asia, 17,300,000 square miles.
Area of Europe, 3,800,000 square miles.
Area of North America, 9,500,000 square miles.
Area of Oceania (incl. Australia) 3,300,000 square miles.
Area of South America, 6,900,000 square miles.
Population of the earth (est.1/1/93), 5,477,000,000.

Principal Islands and Their Areas

Island	Area (Sq.Mi.)
Baffin I., Can.	195,928
Borneo (Kalimantan), Asia	287,300
Celebes (Sulawesi), Indon.	73,057
Corsica, France	3,352
Crete, Greece	3,189
Cuba, N.A.	42,800
Cyprus, Asia	3,572
Great Britain, U.K.	88,795
Greenland, N.A.	840,000
Hainan Dao, China	13,100
Hawaii, U.S.	4,034
Hispaniola, N.A.	29,300
Hokkaidō, Japan	32,245
Honshū, Japan	89,176
Iceland, Europe	39,800
Ireland, Europe	32,600
Jamaica, N.A.	4,200
Java (Jawa), Indon.	51,038
Luzon, Philippines	40,420
Madagascar, Africa	227,000
Mindanao, Philippines	36,537
Newfoundland, Can.	42,031
New Guinea, Oceania	309,000
Puerto Rico, N.A.	3,500
Sakhalin, Russia	29,500
Sardinia, Italy	9,301
Sicily, Italy	9,926
Southampton I., Can.	15,913
Spitsbergen, Norway	15,260
Sri Lanka, Asia	24,900
Taiwan, Asia	13,900
Tasmania, Austl.	26,200
Tierra del Fuego, S.A.	18,600
Vancouver I., Can.	12,079
Victoria I., Can.	83,897

Principal Lakes, Oceans, Seas, and Their Areas

Lake/Country	Area (Sq.Mi.)
Arabian Sea	1,492,000
Arctic Ocean	5,400,000
Atlantic Ocean	31,800,000
Baltic Sea, Eur.	163,000
Bering Sea, Asia-N.A.	876,000
Black Sea, Eur.-Asia	178,000
Caribbean Sea, N.A.-S.A.	1,063,000
Caspian Sea, Asia-Europe	143,240
Chad, L., Cameroon-Chad-Nig.	6,300
Erie, L., Can.-U.S.	9,910
Great Salt Lake, U.S.	1,680
Hudson Bay, Can.	475,000
Huron, L., Can.-U.S.	23,000
Indian Ocean	28,900,000
Mediterranean Sea, Eur.-Afr.-Asia	967,000
Mexico, Gulf of, N.A.	596,000
Michigan, L., U.S.	22,300
North Sea, Eur.	222,000
Ontario, L., Can.-U.S.	7,540
Pacific Ocean	63,800,000
Red Sea, Afr.-Asia	169,000
Superior, L., Can.-U.S.	31,700
Tanganyika, L., Afr.	12,350
Titicaca, Lago, Bol.-Peru	3,200
Victoria, L., Ken.-Tan.-Ug.	26,820
Yellow Sea, China-Korea	480,000

Principal Mountains and Their Heights

Mountain/Country	Elev. (Ft.)
Aconcagua, Cerro, Arg.	22,831
Annapurna, Nepal	26,504
Apo, Mt., Phil.	9,692
Ararat, Turkey	16,804
Blanc, Mont (Monte Bianco), France-Italy	15,771
Bolívar (La Columna), Ven.	16,411
Cameroon Mtn., Cam.	13,451
Chimborazo, Ecuador	20,561
Cook, Mt., New Zealand	12,349
Cristóbal Colón, Pico, Colombia	19,029
Dhaulāgiri, Nepal	26,810
Elbert, Mt., Co., U.S.	14,431
El'brus, Russia	18,510
Elgon, Mt., Kenya-Uganda	14,178
Etna, Mt., Italy	10,902
Everest, Mt., China-Nepal	29,028
Fairweather, Mt., Canada-U.S.	15,300
Fuji-san, Japan	12,388
Gannett Pk., Wy., U.S.	13,785
Gongga Shan, China	24,790
Grand Teton Mtn., Wy., U.S.	13,766
Grossglockner, Austria	12,461
Hood, Mt., Or., U.S.	11,239
Illimani, Nevado, Bol.	21,151
Iztaccíhuatl, Mex.	17,343
Jaya, Puncak, Indon.	16,503
Jungfrau, Switz.	13,642
K2 (Godwin Austen), China-Pak.	28,250
Kānchenjunga, India-Nepal	28,208
Kātrīnā, Jabal, Egypt	8,668
Kenya, Mt., Kenya	17,058
Kilimanjaro, Tanzania	19,340
Kommunizma, Pik, Tajikistan	24,590
Kosciusko, Mt., Austl.	7,316
Koussi, Emi, Chad	11,204
Lassen Pk., Ca., U.S.	10,457
Logan, Mt., Canada	19,524
Longs Pk., Co., U.S.	14,255
Margherita, Zaire-Uganda	16,763
Matterhorn, Italy-Switz.	14,692
Mauna Kea, Hi., U.S.	13,796
Mauna Loa, Hi., U.S.	13,680
McKinley, Mt., Ak., U.S.	20,320
Misti, Volcán, Peru	19,098
Mulhacén, Spain	11,424
Nānga Parbat, Pak.	26,650
Nevis, Ben, U.K.	4,406
Ólimbos, Greece	9,570
Orizaba, Pico de, Mex	18,406
Pikes Pk., Co., U.S.	14,110
Popocatépetl, Volcán, Mex.	17,887
Rainier, Mt., Wa., U.S.	14,410
Sajama, Nevado, Bol.	21,463
Shasta, Mt., Ca., U.S.	14,162
Toubkal, Jebel, Morocco	13,665
Triglav, Slovenia	9,393
Vesuvio (Vesuvius), Italy	4,190
Vinson Massif, Antarc.	16,864
Washington, Mt., N.H., U.S.	6,288
Whitney, Mt., Ca., U.S.	14,491
Wilhelm, Mt., Pap. N. Gui.	14,793

Principal Rivers and Their Lengths

River/Continent	Length (Mi.)
Amazonas–Ucayali, S.A.	4,000
Amu Darya, Asia	1,578
Amur, Asia	2,744
Arkansas, N.A.	1,459
Brahmaputra, Asia	1,770
Colorado, N.A. (U.S.–Mex.)	1,450
Columbia, N.A.	1,200
Congo (Zaïre), Africa	2,900
Danube, Europe	1,776
Euphrates, Asia	1,510
Ganges, Asia	1,560
Huang (Yellow), Asia	3,395
Indus, Asia	1,800
Irrawaddy, Asia	1,300
Lena, Asia	2,700
Limpopo, Africa	1,100
Loire, Europe	625
Mekong, Asia	2,600
Mississippi, N.A.	2,348
Missouri, N.A.	2,315
Murray, Australia	1,566
Negro, S.A.	1,300
Niger, Africa	2,600
Nile, Africa	4,145
Ohio, N.A.	981
Orange, Africa	1,300
Orinoco, S.A.	1,600
Paraguay, S.A.	1,610
Paraná, S.A.	2,800
Peace, N.A.	1,195
Pechora, Europe	1,124
Plata–Paraná, S.A.	3,030
Red, N.A.	1,270
Rhine, Europe	820
Rhône, Europe	500
Rio Grande, N.A.	1,885
Salween (Nu), Asia	1,750
São Francisco, S.A.	1,988
Saskatchewan–Bow, N.A.	1,205
Snake, N.A.	1,038
St. Lawrence, N.A.	800
Sungari (Songhua), Asia	1,140
Syr Dar'ya, Asia	1,370
Tarim, Asia	1,328
Tennessee, N.A.	652
Tigris, Asia	1,180
Tocantins, S.A.	1,640
Ucayali, S.A.	1,220
Ural, Asia	1,509
Uruguay, S.A.	1,025
Volga, Europe	2,194
Xingú, S.A.	1,230
Yangtze (Chang), Asia	3,900
Yellowstone, N.A.	671
Yenisey, Asia	2,543
Yukon, N.A.	1,770
Zambezi, Africa	1,700

Index

Map Names and Abbreviations

This table lists the names and the abbreviations used for features on the physical-political maps. Each entry includes the feature name, the language from which it comes, and in the case of foreign names, its English translation. Abbreviations are shown for those names that are abbreviated on the maps.

Ákra (Greek): cape, *Akr.*
Cabo (Spanish, Portuguese): cape, *C.*
Cap (French): cape, *C.*
Cape (English): *C.*
Cerro (Spanish): mountain, hill
Cordillera (Spanish): mountain chain, *Cord.*
Erg (Arabic): strait
Estrecho (Spanish): strait
Fort (English): *Ft.*
Golfo (Spanish, Italian): gulf, bay, *G.*
Gora (Russian): mountain, *G.*
Gulf (English): *G.*
Hai (Chinese): sea
Île (French): island
Ilha (Portuguese): island
Isla (Spanish) island, *I.*
Jabal (Arabic): mountain
Khrebet (Russian): mountain range
Lake (English): *L.*
Lago (Spanish, Portuguese): lake, *L.*
More (Russian): sea
Mountain(s) (English): *Mt. (Mts.)*
Mys (Russian): cape, *M.*
National (English): *Nat'l.*
Occidental (Spanish): western

Oriental (Spanish): eastern
Óros (Greek): mountain
Ozero (Russian): lake, *Oz.*
Peninsula (English): *Pen.*
Peski (Russian): desert
Plato (Russian): plateau
Point (English): *Pt.*
Pointe (French): point, *Pte.*
Poluostrov (Russian): peninsula, *P-Ov.*
Proliv (Russian): strait
Punta (Spanish): point
Reservoir (English): *Res.*
Río (Spanish): river, *R.*
River (English): *R.*
Salto (Spanish, Portuguese): waterfall
Serra (Portuguese): mountain chain, *Sa.*
Shan (Chinese): mountains
Sierra (Spanish): mountain range, *Sa.*
Sound (English): *Sd.*
Vodokhranilishche (Russian): reservoir, *Vdkhr.*
Volcano (English): *Vol.*

SUMMIT

GLACIER   SNC

TIMBER

HORIZON   ICEBERG

CRATER   DORMANT   ARM
           VOLCANO   TIMBER

OCEAN   ATOLL   FJORD
                              POINT   PLAIN

           STRAIT   BAY
ARCHIPELAGO
                              TOWN
       CHANNEL
                    DELTA

       REEF   SOUND   BLUFF

WAVES   CAPE   SPIT CLIFF   KNOB

                  SANDBAR   GULF   KNOLL   GROVE

SHOAL   INLET BREAKERS BEACH
                                                PASTURE
       PENINSULA   ISTHMUS   LAGOON
HEADLAND   RIVER   BAY
       PRECIPICE
                       SHORE LINE   LEVEE   RAILROAD
BREAKWATER   CITY
                                        AND
       ISLAND   HARBOR WHARF DOCK SEAPORT
                                        BRIDGE
                                 ESTUARY RIVER MOUTH   CULTIVATED LAND
                              PIER

DIKE   AIRPORT

ROAD   HIGHWAY

            FIELD   MEADOW

B-942000-99R-1v-1r-1s-1d